"So many young people are goi[ng] Chasten's words and feel held up otherwise be missing from their community.

—ASHLEY C. FORD,
New York Times bestselling author of *Somebody's Daughter: A Memoir*

"A relatable and heartfelt memoir reminding us all of the beauty and power in being authentically yourself. Sure to make you laugh, cry, and feel deeply inspired."

—RACHAEL LIPPINCOTT and **ALYSON DERRICK,**
New York Times bestselling authors of *She Gets the Girl*

"Told with candor and grace, this . . . is a joyous reminder to be kind to yourself."

—KAL PENN,
bestselling author of *You Can't Be Serious*

"Honest and incredibly moving, *I Have Something to Tell You—For Young Adults* is a deeply relatable story that will resonate with any teen who's searching for their place in this world."

—PHIL STAMPER,
bestselling author of *The Gravity of Us* and *Small Town Pride*

"Buttigieg's voice is clear and honest as he recounts the shame he internalized; his struggle to claim a proud, gay identity; and the challenges he faced while completing his college degree. . . . A hopeful memoir for teens struggling to fit in and feel safe."

—*Kirkus Reviews*

"The vignettes from his youth . . . are entertaining with his flair for humor while simultaneously touching and can help any reader feel not alone. . . . A solid pick for any collection where memoir is popular or any growing LGBTQIA+ collection."

—*SLJ*

I HAVE SOMETHING TO TELL YOU

For Young Adults

A Memoir

CHASTEN BUTTIGIEG

 New York London Toronto Sydney New Delhi

atheneum

An imprint of Simon & Schuster Children's Publishing Division
1230 Avenue of the Americas, New York, New York 10020

This young readers edition is adapted from *I Have Something to Tell You* by Chasten Buttigieg, published by Atria in 2020.

Simon & Schuster: Celebrating 100 Years of Publishing in 2024
For information about special discounts for bulk purchases, please contact Simon & Schuster Special Sales at 1-866-506-1949 or business@simonandschuster.com.
The Simon & Schuster Speakers Bureau can bring authors to your live event. For more information or to book an event, contact the Simon & Schuster Speakers Bureau at 1-866-248-3049 or visit our website at www.simonspeakers.com.
Also available in an Atheneum hardcover edition
Interior design by Irene Metaxatos
The text for this book was set in Aldus LT Std.
Manufactured in the United States of America
First Atheneum paperback edition May 2024
10 9 8 7 6 5 4 3 2 1
The Library of Congress has cataloged the hardcover edition as follows:
Names: Buttigieg, Chasten, 1989– author.
Title: I have something to tell you : a memoir / Chasten Buttigieg.
Other titles: I have something to tell you (Young readers edition)
Description: Young readers edition. | New York : Atheneum, [2023] | Includes bibliographical references. | Audience: Ages 12 up | Audience: Grades 7–9 | Summary: "The young adult adaptation of the moving, hopeful, and refreshingly candid memoir by the husband of former Democratic presidential candidate about growing up gay in his small Midwestern town"— Provided by publisher.
Identifiers: LCCN 2022051573 (print) | LCCN 2022051574 (ebook) | ISBN 9781665904377 (hardcover) | ISBN 9781665904384 (pbk) | ISBN 9781665904391 (ebook)
Subjects: LCSH: Buttigieg, Chasten, 1989—Juvenile literature. | Gay men—Indiana—South Bend—Biography—Juvenile literature. | Presidential candidates' spouses—United States—Biography—Juvenile literature. | Buttigieg, Pete, 1982—Juvenile literature. | South Bend (Ind.)—Biography—Juvenile literature. | Presidents—United States—Election—2020—Juvenile literature.
Classification: LCC F534.S7 B55 2023 (print) | LCC F534.S7 (ebook) | DDC 977.2/890092 [B]—dc23/eng/20221214
LC record available at https://lccn.loc.gov/2022051573
LC ebook record available at https://lccn.loc.gov/2022051574

For every teacher and director who believed in the
scared, confused, and energetic young Chasten who felt
like a square peg in a round world.

For my parents, for loving that little square peg
just the way he was.

For Peter, who pushes me to be a better teacher, husband,
and father in all the best ways.

And for my sweet Penelope and Gus—
I cannot wait to read your stories.

Contents

A Note on Language in My Story

I am so thankful that you've picked up my book. It's a story about a lot of things: growing up, fitting in, fishing, politics, and identity, to name a few. There's a lot of funny stuff in here, but there are also moments that are heartbreaking. And in describing that heartbreak, you may see some words and phrases that you will identify as offputting or hurtful. When these words were used against me, I found them hard to take in as well. I have used them here to tell my story as faithfully as I remember it, even the ugly and painful parts.

While discussing my identity or experience, you may see words or acronyms that you do not use, or that you use differently, and that's okay. Language is always evolving, especially vocabulary within marginalized communities. I want you to know that my goal is to bring people together, never to isolate. That is certainly my wish, and why I am sharing my story. But it is just that—my story. Just one experience among the millions happening around us every day. I hope that by reading about my journey, you will feel compelled to keep sharing yours as authentically as you can.

Foreword by
Ariana DeBose

Before I fully understood and owned my power as an openly queer Afro Latina, I was often the only person who looked like me growing up in a small town in North Carolina. I didn't entirely grasp how I was different, but I liked to think I added some "spice" to the party. From very early on, I loved to dance and sing and entertain people. Performing was the spark at the very center of my heart, and I watched in awe as artists like Rita Moreno, Vanessa Williams, and Gina Torres (artists who, in some way or another, looked like me) dazzled audiences with their singular shine. I wanted to be in the spaces where they stood, and their presence helped me realize that dream was possible.

I am very lucky to have a mother who supports me. As a teacher, she knows how important it is to nurture every child's dream. But it wasn't always easy to navigate situations where I was the only brown person in the room. So, I took what a lot of people might have considered a negative and reframed it as an asset: I realized that being different gave me an incredible strength. It taught me how to listen to others with empathy and compassion, which is an incredibly important act of connection. I also worked *hard*. The barriers of criticism and closed doors occur more frequently and at additional intersections for people from marginalized communities, but I knew I was worthy of being seen and heard.

And then, one day, I found myself standing in the same room as those artists I revered, clutching an Academy Award in my hand. That little girl inside me who had looked up to others for inspiration now looked out at a crowd of people who recognized my spark. That dream might never have materialized if I had decided to keep my head down, to quiet that burning voice inside of me that ached to stand out.

I am honored to take up space unapologetically, because I know firsthand how important it is to see someone who looks like you achieve their dreams. There are still so few examples out there for Afro Latinos or for queer women of color, to name just a few of my communities. I've made it a goal to work with organizations that build safe spaces for young people to explore their unique selves. One such group, Covenant House, provides unhoused youths with the basic human rights necessary to create an environment in which they can thrive. Denying a child the opportunity to explore their identity or their dreams is one of the worst forms of violence, and that is why stories like mine and like Chasten's are so important to tell. Our stories normalize our humanity and add richness to an exquisite, multifaceted spectrum of identities.

The more we speak these stories loudly and proudly and celebrate our differences, the closer we get to accomplishing the beautiful goal of a world based on mutual and human respect. That starts at a foundational level, with our youngest voices—and that's why your story matters too. There are so many outside forces working to make you feel small or strange or unwanted, but I hope that stories like Chasten's, told with care and love, remind you that you are valued, you are not alone, and that acceptance (both self- and community-focused) will find you if you keep looking.

Your story is unique, and that is your *greatest* strength. But—and this is just as important—your differences will connect you to all kinds of beautiful people who are waiting to embrace you and lift you up. Everything that makes you different is a story that is worth being told. I can't wait to see what you have to share.

Introduction:
Everything and Nothing

Revving the engine of her car, Shelly spat out her demands into the Starbucks drive-through speaker box. "I said I wanted more caramel! Make it again!" Just as quickly as she sped off, her brakes shrieked the old pile of steel to a halt as she nearly collided with the car in front of hers. Still only a few feet from the speaker, her voice sent every curse word known to humanity through the cool morning air and into the employees' headsets inside the tiny coffee shop on Kinnickinnic Avenue. We all looked at one another in both horror and amusement and turned the volume on our headsets down as the rant continued. Customers inside could hear her shouting from the drive-through lane and traded sympathetic glances with us as we sped our way through the morning rush hour coffee traffic.

My apron was covered in chocolate sauce and milk splatter, and a hurried pour of coffee missed the cup entirely, sending a stream of the piping hot liquid onto my shoe. I waddled my burning toes back to the counter and called out, "Dark roast for Bill!" Bill rolled his eyes and grabbed the coffee without so much as a "thank you." Impatient and in need of a caffeine fix, Shelly started laying on the horn, upset that her macchiato didn't have enough caramel drizzle and now she was going to be late for work. It was six in the morning, I had been working the morning shift since four, and things weren't going very well for me, my shoe, or Shelly. In a few hours, I'd change my clothes in the bathroom, drive across town, and teach back-to-back theater classes to a group of energetic fourth graders. Suffice it to say, life was chaotic and sticky.

Let's fast-forward eight years. To a different kind of chaos.

It's late evening, and I'm cuddled up on the couch with Buddy, a one-eyed, stinky-breathed mutt, on my lap and my husband at my side in our home in Indiana. My cell phone rings as "Unknown Caller" scrolls across the screen. Whoever is calling doesn't want me to know who they are or what their number is. Intuition told me to answer.

"Hi, is this Chasten?"

"Uh, yes. Who's calling?" I ask.

"Hi, Mr. Buttigieg, I have Jill Biden here to speak with you."

I spring up from the couch and begin to pace around the house, waiting for the former Second Lady, and the (soon to be) First Lady of the United States, Dr. Biden, to come on the phone. My slippers seem to find every creaky board in the old, wooden floors as I walk back and forth, listening to Dr. Biden congratulate me on running a great and historic campaign for president alongside my husband.

Wait. What?!

Yep, you read that right.

In 2018, after three years of dating, I married Pete Buttigieg, who was, at the time, the mayor of South Bend, Indiana, a midsized city about an hour and a half east of Chicago. While the world knows my husband as Mayor Pete, or Secretary Pete, or sometimes even Secretary Mayor Pete, you'll notice I call him Peter, because that's what he goes by to friends and family. I had no idea we'd be celebrating our one-year anniversary on the presidential campaign trail, but just a couple of months after our wedding, Peter and I discussed the idea that he might run for president. I didn't have to think about this choice for a second; I *completely* supported it. As my partner, he had helped me to feel safe and to believe in myself—I knew he could also do that for the rest of the country, and I knew just how important it was for young people to know that there was space for openly gay people to succeed in this country too.

We had no idea the campaign would take off like a

rocket ship. Peter—with the help of hundreds of dedicated, hardworking staff members and thousands of volunteers across the country—ran a campaign of hope, inclusion, and forward-looking progress. About a month before Dr. Biden called, Peter had won the Iowa Caucus, the first contest leading up to the presidential election. It was a big deal and a historic win. Pete was the first gay American to ever win a statewide election in the presidential nominating process. A week after Iowa, he came in a very close second in New Hampshire, but the race shifted after that, and Joe Biden started to become the clear Democratic nominee-to-be. Instead of continuing the campaign, Peter and I made the choice to fly back to South Bend. We gave some teary-eyed speeches on national television, thanked our supporters, and then proudly threw our support behind the Biden campaign. Within a few hours of Pete's campaign winding down, we were at home enjoying some much-needed rest after over a year of living out of suitcases and sleeping on airplanes. Life was changing at a dizzyingly fast pace, and then it suddenly came to a screeching stop.

Now, as I stood in the living room, Dr. Biden continued, "You did something miraculous, something you may not even fully understand the weight of yet. Joe and I are so proud of you and what you have done for this country." I was flattered. I thanked her for her kindness and her time just as she put candidate Biden on the phone. "One heck of a race, man. Really well done. I'm proud of ya," he said. "Is your guy there?" I passed the phone over to Peter and stood dumbfounded in the hallway.

Well, that's one way to end a day!

In just eight years, I went from sleepy and stressful mornings at the coffee shop to crisscrossing the country on a groundbreaking and historic campaign with my husband. Who would have thought that the early mornings and long hours full of complicated coffee orders, as well as an unpredictable and demanding teaching schedule, would prepare me for working on a presidential campaign? I never saw all this change coming. Never planned for it. Never calculated my decisions in order to get me to this point. I never thought in a million years that I would be on television, in the newspapers, and on the stage helping deliver a message of hope and inclusion that I wished I could've experienced when I was younger.

When we launched Peter's campaign, I hadn't thought about what role *I* would need to play on the trail. Which is exactly the point: political spouses must be both everything and nothing, working nonstop without ever stealing the spotlight. "There's only one star," I had been repeatedly told, "and it's not you." At the same time, the spouse plays a crucial role in front of the cameras and behind the scenes. You know the candidate the best. You know what keeps them energized, especially when they're running on two hours of sleep and have to go into their sixth interview of the day. You show up when the candidate can't be there, and you fill in all the gaps. Sometimes this means delivering speeches in front of big crowds or handling last-minute television interviews, and it always means keeping exactly the right expression on your face and landing all of your talking points. You never know who's recording or taking a photo or listening to your phone call. You're required to be known as "the candidate's spouse" at the very minimum, but you're expected to do, and *be*, a *lot* more than that.

In a way, this "everything and nothing" role reminded me a lot of the experience of figuring out who I was when I was younger—blending in, making friends, assessing how far I could stick my neck out or how much space I could take up, all the while coming to terms with my identity as a gay man. *Make sure you say the right thing. Do the right thing, always. Don't be an embarrassment. Make people proud. Don't get in the way.* The pressure on the campaign was heavy and ever present, but what made it so much easier than a childhood of hiding my true self was that once I was on national television with my husband, I wasn't scared of who I was. In fact, over the years, I'd learned that what I was hiding shouldn't be hidden at all. I had embraced who I was and gave myself permission to live a truly authentic, unashamed, and proud life, regardless of what other people thought of me, my marriage, and my family.

Running for president is hard work. Beyond the brutal schedule and the high stakes, I wasn't prepared for what having to exist in public would do to me, the stress it would put on my family and friends, or the weight that being every-thing for everyone all the time would have on my mental health. I didn't know just how terrible and invasive people could be on the internet—and I especially wasn't prepared for the threats of violence. When you're on the national stage, it can feel as if everything you do, everywhere you go, and everything you say is being examined through a magni-fying glass. When you're campaigning, most people only get to know you through what they read about you online or see in brief interview clips. Sometimes they'll make assumptions about you simply because of who you are married to. Having a strong sense of self and moral compass helped me stay true to myself during the campaign, but I didn't always have that strength and confidence when I was younger.

I've been given incredible opportunities that I wouldn't trade for anything. Having a platform to shape conversa-tions and influence change is a tremendous privilege! I didn't believe I could do that at first, but the more time I spent out on the campaign trail, the more I realized that the experi-ences and memories I was scared of, embarrassed of, or had kept hidden weren't as weird to discuss as I'd assumed they'd be. They were just real: the true Chasten. Even more amaz-ing, people seemed to appreciate hearing about them and often could relate to them.

The fact is, my story isn't rare. It's actually pretty com-mon: I grew up in a conservative small town, with loving parents who worked hard to support me but didn't know many gay people before I came out to them when I was eighteen, terrified that they would reject me. Even after I came out, I couldn't shake the feeling that this essential part of me meant I'd never find love or have a family. Despite being an overachieving high school student and working multiple jobs, I struggled to finish college, and I graduated with a lot of student debt. I spent years desperately looking for some sign of a happy, stable future. I even experienced housing insecurity for a time, and my struggles with mental health and identity meant I often questioned if I was going to make it to the next day. It took a lot of hard work, but, as RuPaul says, "If you can't love yourself, [how] ya gonna love anybody else?" I had to learn to love myself and trust that the rest would follow.

I was never very interested in politics while I was in school, and I definitely never thought I'd find myself involved in conversations about the future of our country! But my experiences on the campaign trail, meeting people across the country and talking to both politicians and constituents, have shown me that being involved in politics is about a lot more than the laws, rights, and governing bodies that make up the United States. The issues surrounding politics are in all our living rooms. They're around our kitchen tables and in our mailboxes. Whether I was hearing the stories of young LGBTQ+ people who'd been kicked out of their homes and didn't know what to do next or talking to teachers who felt they weren't getting the support they needed, I was constantly reminded that Americans should be able to see themselves in the people representing them at the highest levels of government.

We're currently living through enormous political and social changes, both in our country and all over the world. The choices and actions we make every day affect the environment, global health, the economy, and our fellow citizens' human and civil rights. I think Peter and I are part of a group of young politicians and activists who can reexamine the way we all live and interact with one another—and the world. I loved being a middle school teacher, and even though I'm not in the classroom every day, there's still a lot of work to be done that asks all of us to roll up our sleeves and get involved. I don't want to waste the chance I've been given to be a part of some of the most important conversations we're having as a country and community.

From growing up raising cows in small-town America to being the other half of a historic presidential campaign, life has taken a lot of twists and turns and taught me quite a few lessons along the way. I certainly haven't figured it all out yet, but I'm eager to share my journey and those lessons with you. I hope the stories within these pages either hold up a mirror to your own experiences and help you feel less alone or offer you a way to think differently about your place in the world and how you relate to it. Either way, I'm excited to do it together.

1

There Are No Sharks in Lake Michigan

When I was a kid, teachers used to tell my parents that I was "special" or "unique." At parent-teacher conferences, they'd say things like, "Well, he sure is . . . eccentric" or "You know, he's just not like the other boys." I thought these comments were a good thing, and seeing as I never heard these words used to describe my two older brothers, they built up my confidence. Then, around middle school, I began to realize that in addition to being creative, getting good grades, and having a knack for making people laugh, I was also gay.

Once I started to put the pieces of my identity together, a battle broke out in my head. What I had been taught about gay people from a young age, what kids my age were saying about gay people, and what I felt in my heart began fighting and tearing me apart.

I was told being gay was a choice, a sin, and an embar-rassment. Of course these things aren't true, but younger Chasten didn't know that. Back then, the outside world was telling me otherwise, and I spent years believing there was no future in store for me. Childhood was fairly sunny and easy. However, once this piece of my identity became clearer, hiding it felt like concealing a giant, glittered, fanged beast inside my stomach. One simple slip and the beast would come tearing through my guts, flop onto the floor in front of the classroom, and shout, *HE'S GAAAAAAAY!* as the entire classroom pointed and laughed in the most humiliating way. In order to keep the beast quiet, I paid very close attention to the way I walked, talked, and acted, because the world just wasn't ready to accept LGBTQ+ people as equals (yet).

My parents had always encouraged me to be myself, but I knew that meant the version of myself that fit the norm. At the time, growing up in a politically and religiously conserva-tive place like Northern Michigan meant that being straight was the only thing you could openly and safely identify as. There wasn't much room for difference. A lot of people back then (and, sadly, some people to this day) believe that being gay is a choice and that all LGBTQ+ people deserve to be mocked, harmed, or worse. Some politicians still use harmful tropes to advocate against protections for LGBTQ+ people.

I knew that being gay meant I'd rather have a boyfriend than a girlfriend. Other than that, I was confused as to why the world thought that made me so different from everyone else, but I didn't have anyone I could talk to about it. I didn't have any gay role models, I never saw myself reflected in the characters I read about in books, and there weren't many characters in movies or television shows living a happy, gay life.

In 1998, when I was nine years old and just starting to understand what these questions swirling around in my head meant, a show called *Will & Grace* aired on television. It featured two gay characters navigating work, life, and love in New York City. Not only did it show me for the first time that there were other people like me out there, but the show had a huge audience! Sure, it had its fair share of backlash for featuring gay people, but the show was winning awards and receiving good ratings. I remember my fear of laughing too enthusiastically whenever actor Sean Hayes's hilarious, very outrageous character, Jack, dramatically and loudly entered the room. If anyone heard how happy the show made me, would they think I was gay? The few times I did watch the show in front of my family, it was both torture *and* therapy. I loved seeing someone "like me" on TV, but I was nervous for anyone to notice that I loved it. I wished that I could live somewhere like New York City, where it would be okay to be like someone on *Will & Grace*, where I could find friends who would be kind to someone "like that."

Then, in 2003, comedian Ellen DeGeneres started her own talk show, *Ellen*. A few years earlier in 1997, DeGeneres came out as gay. The show she was starring in at the time was promptly canceled, and Ellen struggled to find any work in Hollywood, just because she'd had the courage to come "out of the closet." Eventually, she was given her own talk show, but she wasn't allowed to talk about her partner or being gay at all. She was even advised not to wear jeans because they could make her "look gay." How exhausting!

Ellen's show was always on when I came home from school, and watching her make my mom laugh hinted to me that there might be a future where all LGBTQ+ people could do great things, be whoever they wanted to be, and not be seen as unusual. For a long time, Ellen was the only LGBTQ+ person I knew about. Even though I saw a few gay characters on television, gayness was something distant, almost like a luxury or a privilege. Famous people on television in Los Angeles or New York could be gay, but not an awkward kid from the Midwest who spent his Saturdays at the bowling alley and read books with a flashlight under the covers. It felt as if growing up somewhere like Northern Michigan meant it was impossible that I could be gay—gay people weren't found in places like that!

I had no idea that just sixteen years after *Ellen* aired its first episode, I would be flying to Los Angeles to be on the other side of the audience, talking about the first version of this book, and reflecting on the fact that my husband had just finished a strong and groundbreaking campaign to be president of the United States of America.

As I stood backstage at the *Ellen* show, a woman quickly

blotted my nose with a little more powder, checked my outfit, and told me to listen for the cue.

"Please welcome my friend Chasten Buttigieg!" Ellen
announced. The sound of applause filled the television
studio, and I stepped out into the bright lights, all cameras
pointed at me. I was thrilled that someone I had looked up
to as a kid was saying my name. Best of all, she said it right!

Yeah, what's up with the name? you're probably asking.
Okay, let's get this out of the way, shall we? The last name
Buttigieg (pronounced "BOOT-uh-jej") is Maltese (from a
small group of islands in the middle of the Mediterranean).
My husband's father immigrated to the United States from
Malta in the 1970s, and I liked the name, so I decided to
take it when we got married. These days, Buttigieg is the
name that gets recognized (you know, that whole husband-
running-for-president thing), and it's my uncommon first
name that typically confuses people. Pete Buttigieg's husband? What's his name? It's not uncommon for me to have
to repeat my name over and over again at the coffee counter
until it is ultimately shouted back as "Chastain," "Justin,"
or "Charles."

Chasten ("CHASS-ten"; rhymes with CLASS-ten) is a
difficult name on the first try, but I've grown to appreciate
it over the years. It's usually, for better or worse, one of the
first things people ask me about when we're introduced. I
didn't appreciate my name's uniqueness until later in life.
I've never met another Chasten, but when I was younger,

my name was just another thing that made me stick out. Kids can be cruel for no reason, and my name was an easy target. One of my worst bullies used to call me "Chasteen" and "Chastity" at the back of the school bus. Now that I'm older, I think about how lonely or sad that bully must have been to not have had anything better to do but make fun of somebody's *name*. I've found that most people who are making fun of others usually have something else going on in their life that causes them to lash out. Rarely is whatever a bully has decided to focus on ever about the person being bullied (though that doesn't justify the behavior!). In this case, I guess Chasten was just *too* unique for Becky on the bus.

When I walked across the stage at my high school graduation, my name was announced as Chase-tin J. Gleeze-man (it's actually Glezman). My cheeks burned red with shame. Even at seventeen, I was still embarrassed of my name. *Oh, come on!* I thought. After all those years at school, they still couldn't get it right? Correctly pronouncing someone's name is an easy way to show them that they are valued. (Similarly, don't be afraid to correct someone if they don't address you the way you prefer. And if anyone has an issue with being asked to do the bare minimum, like I said, it's a reflection on them, not you. Sometimes, rather than working on themselves, people will channel their anger and confusion into hurting others, even with small things like names.) On the bright side, at least high school was over when they butchered my name onstage, right?

Mysteriously, the story of how I got this unique name is inconclusive; there is an answer, but it's an incomplete one. My mom used to take on shifts as a nursing assistant at our local hospital in addition to managing our family's landscaping business, and she swears that a woman she worked with at the hospital was putting on a Christmas play that featured a character named King Chasten. As soon as she heard that name, she loved it. Of course, I've done extensive research, and I can't find a King Chasten anywhere. As I've said, I'm very mysterious.

Regardless, it's not pronounced like the verb, which means "to have a restraining effect on" and which is the opposite of my usually peaceful, nonbossy personality (at least I hope). It's pronounced with a short *a* and a hard *t*: CHASS-ten.

If anything, my name is an expression of my parents' creativity. My mom and dad, Sherri and Terry Glezman, are loving, dedicated people who live for their friends and family; they always made sure their three children's lives were full of little adventures (and some bigger ones). The way they raised us was neither hands-off nor controlling, which allowed me to develop my independence in a genuine way without feeling totally on my own or without good guidance. Though we've had our hard times, certain phrases ring true: my parents always "wanted the best for me," and they absolutely "made me who I am today." Since understanding that is part of the point of writing a memoir, family is where I must begin.

My grandparents planted permanent roots in Traverse City, Michigan (population 15,559 as of 2022), in 1959, when my grandfather was relocated as part of his service in the US Coast Guard. Since then, the extended family nearby has grown so large that we can't fit into a single house for our holiday gatherings. Instead, we now squeeze close to forty people at a time into my father's finished barn. The woods and waters of Northern Michigan provided a lot of necessary set elements for my "go rub some dirt in it, you'll be fine" childhood. Our family now splits our time between Michigan and Washington, D.C., and every time I come back to the Midwest, I am reminded just how special our little slice of paradise is.

Traverse City is surrounded by an abundance of nature. We have four distinct seasons here, each full of its own unique charms. Although a lot of locals will tell you the winter is the longest and worst season, I appreciate the variety, and my parents made sure each season was as special as possible. The woods are dense and lush green, perfect for hide-and-seek and building forts out of fallen trees and branches. Michigan is surrounded by four of the Great Lakes, Lake Michigan being the closest to Traverse City. (If you hold up your right hand with your palm facing you, it looks like the Lower Peninsula of Michigan, which is why we're called the "Mitten State." Traverse City would be near the tip of your pinky, and Lake Michigan touches everything on the left side of your hand map.) The water is fresh (meaning no sharks!), and some of the lakes are so clear and turquoise blue that you can see fifty feet or more to the bottom. At least, that's what it's like in warmer weather; when it's cold, the lakes freeze over. Which means in the summer, you've got fishing, and in the winter, there's . . . ice fishing. Luckily, there is always an abundance of wildlife roaming around "Up North." We typically see deer and turkeys in our backyard, and it's not uncommon for the occasional black bear to wreak havoc on birdfeeders, garbage cans, or campers' coolers.

The weather in Northern Michigan brings out the best and worst of every season. There are harsh and freezing-cold snowstorms in the winter that occasionally pile snow so high, you can't open your front door. We had a lot of canceled school days when I was a kid, which were typically spent outside making snowmen, sledding, and digging snow forts with Dad into the side of the hill in front of our home. After hours in the snow, when we could no longer feel our toes, Mom would call us in for hot chocolate and chicken noodle soup, just like in the commercials. As the snowplow truck finally reached our neighborhood to clear the roads, signaling that we'd probably have to go back to school the next day, we'd shout our displeasure from the frosted windows. One winter, my dad, with help from a few neighbors, built an ice-skating rink in our backyard using a tarp, a garden hose, and some cheap lumber. We'd spend all day on the ice and even shine lights on it at night, devoting every moment we could to skating and playing hockey until the ice finally began to melt in the spring.

The summers in Northern Michigan are perfect, just hot enough for a day at the beach. We have so many lakes in Michigan that the rule of thumb says you're never more than six miles from water. And in the fall (arguably my favorite season and not because I'm unapologetically obsessed with pumpkin spice lattes), the temperature dips into "sweater weather" and the leaves on the trees burst into red, yellow, and orange hues.

My dad leaned into every season. He especially loved decorating our house for Halloween and Christmas, and helping him became one of my favorite traditions. In the fall, we'd go to a farmstand and pick out buckets of apples for Mom to make pies and applesauce with, and we'd select our perfect pumpkins for carving. (I was always a fan of the bumpy, misfit pumpkins that nobody else seemed to like—I wonder why!) Dad covered every inch of our front porch with cobwebs, hay bales, and cornstalks. We'd build coffins out of plywood that my dad would jump out of to scare trick-or-treaters, and one year, Dad set up a zip line from the roof to the big tree in our front yard to swing a ghost across, scaring little candy-seeking ghouls and sending them running back to their parents' arms. Just a few weeks later, as winter started to peek around the corner, Dad and I would ensure every tree and window had Christmas lights on them. There were a few years when my parents made us wear snowsuits under our Halloween costumes, so Dad and I made sure Christmas decorations were up before Thanksgiving, in case early snowfalls made it too hard to decorate outside.

Spending time outside was important to my parents. They often valued playing outside more than reading indoors. The best example of the kind of rough-and-tumble, free-spirited childhood I had happened at Fish Camp. What's Fish Camp, you ask? Well, Fish Camp was *the* annual father-son tradition in our family. And it all centered around— you guessed it—fishing. My mother's uncle, Uncle Gene, has a cabin far out in the middle of nowhere in the Upper Peninsula of Michigan. For those of you unfamiliar with the great state of Michigan, the Upper Peninsula ("the U.P." or, as us Michiganders call it, "the Yoop") is the northernmost and mostly rural portion of the state that hunters and vacationers all enjoy equally. Remember the hand map? There's a stretch of land northwest of the mitten, separated by Lakes Michigan and Huron. Use your left hand to visualize it, palm facing you, with your thumb pointing up and your fingers running horizontally. Fish Camp is at the corner where your left hand's thumb and pointer finger meet, at the same latitude as Quebec, Canada—way up there!

Every summer, my dad, my two older brothers, and I would make the journey to the U.P. together. The four of us would pile into Dad's truck and make the seven-hour drive north with a truckload of coolers camping gear, and a bag full of Dad's homemade beef jerky. Along the way, Dad would stop at the Mackinac Bridge—the suspension bridge that connects Michigan's Upper and Lower Peninsulas (aka your right and left hands; I won't let the hand map go, I am so sorry)—so we could take in the view and buy a pop from the convenience store. We'd play car games across the U.P., listening to talk radio or the local country music station, until the only signs of civilization were the occasional pasty stand (a meat pie native to the U.P.), fish bait shop, or gas station (which most likely sold pasties *and* bait).

Once we made it to Baraga (with a population of less than two thousand), we'd stop and say hi to Uncle Gene and "Aunty Mares"—that's Aunt Marilyn in "Yooper" speak. (Folks who live in the U.P. call themselves "Yoopers," and Yoopers call everyone who lives south of, or "under," the Mackinac Bridge "Trolls." Get it? We're a fun people.) Yoopers have a thick, unique northern accent, some of which has rubbed off on my family over the years. Once, during a college theater production, the director kept stopping the rehearsal to make me repeat the line "Oh my God" *properly*, since I apparently kept saying "Oh my Ged." Every student watching in the audience was laughing hysterically as I kept repeating the line over and over until the director threw her hands in the air, gave up, and left the stage in a huff. It took me a long time to hear the difference. Most of my Michigan accent has stuck with me, especially my overuse of the expression "ope!" (which is usually used to mean "excuse me" or "wow" or "oops" or "oh no she didn't!").

Uncle Gene had the thickest Yooper accent of all. Waving from his front porch, he'd see us off to camp while shouting something like, "Hey! Dem skeeters are bitin' real hard—make sure ya ladder on da bug dope." (That's, uh, "The mosquitos are real bad, so be sure to wear plenty of bug spray, dontcha know.") A few more miles into the forest was where the real adventure began. Dad would park the truck at the camp gate, and we'd throw on our backpacks, strap the coolers and fishing gear down onto an ATV, and complete the journey into camp on a small two-track trail littered with potholes and covered in tree trunks left over from the last thunderstorm. The act of parking the truck, throwing on your backpack, and trudging through the rich, copper mud was thrilling. You truly felt cut off from the rest of the world. Before cell phones, we'd call home from Uncle Gene's house and let Mom know we'd made it to Baraga, and then she wouldn't hear from us for a week until we reemerged from the woods and arrived back at Uncle Gene's for a much-needed shower and a phone call home.

There was no electricity or running water in the cabin. And, not that we ever needed it when I was a kid, but no Wi-Fi, either! In the daytime, in addition to fishing, we'd practice shooting clay pigeons or targets with rifles Dad brought. I became a good marksman, even though I was always uncomfortable around guns. I never really warmed up to handling something that could hurt me or someone else. I knew I could make mistakes fishing, but those mistakes most likely wouldn't kill me! Guns made my stomach queasy. I always handled them with care and extreme focus, and of course Dad would have never let me be irresponsible with them, but I never felt at ease during target practice. Shooting guns was anxiety-inducing for me, rather than a fun and relaxing activity with the guys. Seeing the gun cases set out on the picnic table made me nervous, and although my dad has gifted me a few guns for birthdays over the years, they remain in his safe back home.

Dad took gun safety very seriously, and he prided himself on teaching his three boys responsibility in every sense. He taught us how to clean a gun, carry a gun, and safely use a gun. This became something I could discuss with many voters on the campaign trail who had strong concerns about gun safety and ownership or their right to own guns, including sharing my own experiences as a teacher having to run lockdown drills with my middle schoolers in a new age of terrifying gun violence. Although I have different political opinions from some gun owners about the need for guns, I am glad my dad showed me that there are gun owners who take responsibility and care very seriously. I just don't want to own one.

My favorite part of Fish Camp wasn't shooting; it was the fish. Evenings were spent cooking what we'd caught that day. Dad would send me to pump water from the well, then we would fillet and clean the fish, toss them in some batter we had brought from home, and fry them in a skillet over the campfire. Sometimes while Dad was gutting the fish, he'd brag to everyone that he had caught the biggest fish that day, and we'd immediately plunge into a playful argument over whose fish was biggest. Dad would pull each fish out of the bucket and compliment the fisherman. "All right, Chasten! Look at this one!" I know, it's just a fish, but Dad's compliments always built me up.

I always felt closest to Dad at camp, and moments like these dinners around the fire, when oftentimes it was just him and me preparing a meal off the bed of his pickup truck, made me feel especially helpful and important to him. The simplicity was remarkable. The sun would set, we'd build a bonfire and grill some fish, and Uncle Gene would drive out to camp to tell us scary stories about man-eating wolves, close encounters with bears, and the occasional camper-abducting alien. Once the fire died down, we'd be left in the darkness with a night sky full of stars so spectacularly vivid, it felt as if you could reach your hand out and scoop them out of thin air.

We slept in sleeping bags on bunk beds made out of old lumber, with Dad sleeping closest to the cabin door with a gun propped up near his bed just in case a bear or wolf came too close to camp. This was done for safety, but also, I'm convinced, just to scare the bejesus out of me. Right when I'd start to doze off, my dad would say something like, "Shh! Did you hear that?" I'd sit up, fumble for my glasses, and turn on my flashlight. There was nothing outside, of course, and Dad couldn't keep himself from snickering. My brothers would join in, which made falling asleep that much harder—not only was I scared, but I was usually embarrassed, too.

Fish Camp was supposed to be a time to demonstrate my masculinity and my ability to "man up" (whatever that means). But then you would hear the mice tearing into the Pop-Tarts left out on the counter and try your best not to squirm while they feasted a few feet from your head, which I suppose wasn't seen as particularly "manly" either. It was never a question of *if* there were mice in the cabin, just . . . *where*. I'd try my best to hide my squeamishness and fear from the rest of the cabin. My two older brothers were much closer with each other, and as the odd one out, I was an easy target for a quick laugh. Not that I didn't get my brothers back, though. Just as things were quieting down, I'd tap my fingers on the wall of the cabin to make it sound like a mouse was crawling up the wall. Whoever was on the top bunk usually fell for it.

I always prided myself on my performance at Fish Camp—throughout my childhood and adolescence, I was driven by a desire to do well. Not because I loved fishing or whatever competition I was in: I mostly wanted to prove to my parents and brothers that I wasn't a wimp and that I could do hard things on my own. Especially the things I knew they couldn't. We were a competitive family, and putting my best foot forward, both to win and to impress my parents, was always the name of the game. Whether it was a game of Monopoly or volleyball, if there was a hint of competition, then we were all in it to win it.

Back home, my older brothers were Dad's boys, always fixing cars or lawn mowers or up early in the mornings to hunt with him, while I usually ran errands and spent more time with Mom, tending to the house and poring over my homework. I was secretly very good at a lot of things involving the Great Outdoors, but there was no getting past the fact that my brothers and I were just very different from one another. I sometimes wondered how my parents had had them and then me. They didn't seem to like me occupying any of their spaces, and the spaces I occupied—like the library, the bowling alley, and the stage—didn't make any sense to them. While I was typically following the rules, mostly out of fear of sticking out too much, my brothers were more comfortable pushing the boundaries and getting into trouble, sometimes in pretty complicated or unusual ways.

This sense of adventure and fearlessness usually peaked at Fish Camp. There was the time they almost started a forest fire because one of them had stepped on a ground nest of bees, gotten stung, and decided that they needed to go back to the scene of the crime with a gallon of gasoline and a blowtorch to seek revenge. This came to my attention when my oldest brother zoomed into camp on a four-wheeler and jumped off so fast that the ATV kept rolling for a few more yards. Just as a small plume of smoke became visible on the horizon, Dad came rushing out of the cabin, grabbed a jug of water and a shovel, jumped onto another ATV, and zipped off into the woods. It was a small fire that was easy to put out, and thankfully, the forest was saved. My brothers had a good laugh, but Dad was furious. While Dad raced to clean up their mess, I remained in my folding chair next to the cabin, reading my books and enjoying an ice-cold Barq's root beer.

Fishing was where I excelled. Was it my favorite thing in the world? Far from it. Was I good at it and did I therefore try my best to outperform everyone else because of this? Of course. I was a confident fisherman, great at tying hooks, and never minded getting my hands dirty or slimy. This quality later helped me succeed equally well at raising cows and, eventually, at handling our newborn twins with a lot of dirty diapers and spit-up. One of my brothers, however, hated touching worms and putting them on the hook. I knew if I acted the way he did when handling a little earthworm, I wouldn't have heard the end of it. There would have been dramatic reenactments of the shrieking and complaining that night around the fire. If I were to point it out, though, I'd probably get a tough-love smack on the shoulder and be told to "shut up." There were peculiar boundaries when it came to who got to poke fun at whom and for what.

The crown jewel of Fish Camp brags came one summer when my dad, a few hundred yards down the river and cussing so loud that the fish probably covered their ears, lost his favorite lure after his line snapped while reeling in a strong fish; about an hour later, I caught an impressive largemouth bass. The catch was so impressive that Uncle Gene had to set his line down and come take a picture of it on my disposable, waterproof camera. "Holy wah! We bedder measure it up and tell da DNR, eh? Dat's gotta be a Michigan record right der, Chassin!" When we finally got back to the cabin and began gutting it for dinner, there, lodged deep in the fish's throat, was Dad's favorite lure. I was really pleased with what this said about my fishing skills, though of course I never would have said that out loud.

Just kidding. Everyone hears this story . . . annually, at every family gathering.

My dad is a no-nonsense kind of guy, reserved but very funny in his own way. He's stout, not too tall, but sturdy, with a trimmed mustache and a shaved head. He had high, unspoken expectations of me, but most people know him for his gentle spirit, generosity, and love of surprises and scares. It's not hard to go about town and run into someone who knows my dad. They'll tell me about the kind favors he has done for them, like plowing snow off their driveway early in the morning before they need to get to work or springing into action to help fix an appliance or a burst pipe. Dad will always drop whatever he is doing to help someone else. It's always a pleasure to hear my dad laugh because it rarely happens, but when it does, especially when he's really proud of his tomfoolery, it's hard not to laugh with him.

When I was young, I thought I was his easiest target,

but now I wonder if he played tricks on me so much because he thought the opposite. Maybe he saw pranks as tests and learning opportunities for me, or gifts that told me he trusted me and that he knew I wouldn't set anything on fire. I wonder if my dad knew that I could handle a challenge, that I was up for the push? I knew he wanted me to be strong, brave, confident, and trustworthy. I think Dad saw something unique in me, something that set me apart from my brothers, and he knew I needed a different kind of guidance from what he offered them. Deep down, Dad knew I was more sensitive than my brothers, and he wanted to protect me in his own way, even if it often went unspoken.

Some examples of Dad's loving pranks: In the summers, he would take us out on the lake on our small pontoon boat, and after I watched the classic man-eating shark movie *Jaws*—at way too young an age—he would swim under the boat and pull my legs from below so that I thought I was being attacked by a shark. (There, uh, are no sharks in Lake Michigan.) At Fish Camp, our usual fishing hole was a big, muddy, tree-lined riverbank; if you navigated the mud well, you could wade out into the slow-moving river all the way up to your chest. One year, a sturgeon jumped out of the water about fifty yards down from where I was standing in the middle of the river. I'd never seen a fish that big before (they can grow up to eight feet long), and my dad shouted from downstream, "Get out of the water! They'll eat your legs!" You'd think that, as a teenager, I'd have been able to recognize when he was teasing me, but when it came to monsters in the water, I never took my chances. I waded as fast as I could out of the river, and my dad couldn't stop laughing. My scream was most definitely heard from miles away.

Unfortunately, autumn didn't offer young Chasten a break. Every year around Halloween, WTCM, the local country radio station in Northern Michigan, would play a Halloween song called "The Legend," which said with frightening detail that every seven years a creature that was half man, half vicious dog (but not a werewolf?)—and was known as the "Dogman"—roamed Northern Michigan towns, terrorizing farm animals and tearing apart its victims. (*Every year*, the song would say, "The seventh year is here.") Whenever the song came on, even though my dad knew I hated it, he would crank the volume up, rolling down the windows and howling as I pleaded with him to cut it out. When we went camping, he'd ask me as we walked through the woods, "Chasten, do you think the Dogman is out?" or whisper, "The seventh year is here," and I'd grip my flashlight tighter as Dad cackled.

This particular torture reached its peak one Halloween when he put on a wolf mask, scaled a ladder up to my bedroom window, and scratched at the screen. When I woke up, I thought I saw the Dogman glaring at me from outside. My bedroom was right next to the back porch, so by the time I'd jumped out of bed and sprinted to the living room, the

Dogman had also shifted positions and was visible outside the porch door. The Dogman was wearing my dad's clothes, but that didn't reassure me at all. I thought he very well may have eaten my dad already, then put on his clothes. That's a thing that *absolutely* could've happened. Hearing her son screaming bloody murder, my mom came rushing in, at which point my dad opened the door and took off his wolf mask. Mom was livid, but Dad, of course, could barely contain himself. He still calls me, every Halloween, to play the song through the phone whenever he hears it on the radio. If it's the month of October and Dad is calling after five p.m., I have to think twice about answering my phone. I still hate the Dogman, and I'm still suspicious of open water.

The most educational of Dad's pranks took place at Fish Camp when I was about thirteen. From the cabin, we'd take our four-wheelers through the woods, following two or three trails my uncle had cleared or mapped for us, until we emerged at the river. From there, we'd walk along the steep riverbank until we found a spot we liked, miles from another human being. The silence was peaceful, but it was also a reminder of how far away from everything we truly were.

One day at camp, my brothers wanted to go to a different fishing hole than the one we'd ended up at, so my dad agreed to find a new location with them. Dad made sure I was fine to stay where I was alone and said he'd come back to pick me up in a little bit. They all rode off on their four-wheelers, and I settled in for a solitary span of fishing. The sun was shining, the birds were chirping, and I was more than happy to be alone. As I believe I mentioned, I was a skilled fisherman—I didn't need someone to babysit me.

Some time passed, longer than necessary to drop my brothers off and come back, but it was still daylight, so I wasn't too worried. I just kept fishing. But then the sun began to set, and I started getting worried. I pride myself on having inherited my father's excellent sense of direction, but I wasn't sure walking miles alone through the woods in the dark was the wisest choice (again, I was thirteen). My mind started racing: *What if it rains? What if Dad never comes back? What if I die at the age of thirteen on a rocky riverbank surrounded by nothing but mosquitoes and half-eaten Cheez-Its?!* I had been confident in my abilities to survive while the sun was up. I had water, food, and an eye on the horizon. Besides, monsters come out only at night, right? I mean, the song never mentioned the Dogman walking the woods looking for kids to eat during the *day*!

Dad had never told us what to do if we found ourselves alone in the middle of the forest at night. What I did know was that I had waterproof matches in my tackle box and how to start a fire, so that's what I did. I continued fishing to keep busy, but as the sun started to disappear behind the tree line and the sky was getting darker and darker, the fear really started to set in. A few hours had passed. Was my dad lost? Bleeding on the ground in front of a hungry bear? Had the giant fish ghost who haunted the riverbank snatched him up and led him to a watery grave? Eventually, I packed up my tackle box and turned my back to the river, figuring the monsters—except for the fish ghost—would come from the woods. Now I was worried. Even more than worried, I was mad. Why hadn't Dad come back? Why would he leave me? Across the river was a steep bank, and the woods rose above me by about a hundred feet. Surely the wolves were perched there, watching.

Finally, I heard a four-wheeler in the distance. The moment Dad came into the clearing, I was running to him, asking why he had left me for so long. Before he could turn the engine off, I was shouting. I must have sounded like a parent myself: How could he do such a thing? Didn't he love me? Why would he abandon me in the middle of the forest? Leaving his own child to fend for himself in the middle of the woods at night? I could have been eaten! BY THE DOGMAN! (Maybe this one was a little less than parental.) It turned out that Dad had been on the other side of the river the entire time, watching to see what I'd do.

Dad believed in pushing us out of the nest to see if we could fly. Like it or not, I'd extended my wings and flown. Riding back to camp, I was fuming. I couldn't look at him, I was so mad—I felt like he had broken my trust. It took me years to understand how much he had trusted me and what that lesson meant to both of us. He wasn't trying to hurt my feelings or scare me; he was simply testing me because he thought I was mature enough to be tested.

Mom still gives Dad a lot of grief for the tricks he played on me when I was younger, but when I tell the story of Dad leaving me in the woods, she seems more proud than protective. I think she knew he had done right by her and me, making sure I could take care of myself. I was going to be all right. I always felt closer to him on those trips—he gave me more than enough room to explore and be myself, without ever actually causing me harm.

At home, things felt different. Dad was back to working long days on landscaping jobs around the area, so he came home tired; he had a lot of responsibilities both at home and at work as a small business owner. When we were at camp, Dad leaned into every adventure, even the most mundane, like lying on the picnic table looking up the stars or roasting marshmallows over the campfire. Back home, Dad tried his best to stay awake at the dinner table while talking to my brothers about football or hockey. When the conversation turned to me, I usually told him about something I was reading or a fun fact about geography. He'd act interested because he knew I was. As a father myself now, looking back at everything he was trying to do for everyone, I realize he must've been exhausted all the time.

While my dad took it upon himself to teach us how to trust our instincts and fend for ourselves (safely and responsibly!), my mom, Sherri, taught us the value of routine and reward. She is joyfully loud—in the best way—and wonderfully eccentric. She has jet-black hair that's often expertly held in place with a whole lot of hair spray. (I remember as a kid waiting on Mom to get ready to leave—you knew it was almost time to go when you heard the sound of aerosol coming out of the can.) She wears a necklace and bracelet with individual charms that correspond to each of her children and grandchildren. When she used to yell our names, it was often so loud and insistent, you'd think there was a serious emergency: a large object about to fall and crush her or a pet-related tragedy. Usually, she just wanted help carrying groceries into the house. She's never afraid to dance or sing in front of strangers, even if she doesn't know the words or have the right moves, and she loves to host family and friends, which means she always wanted the house in perfect shape. In a very mom way, she decorated our kitchen with those wall hangings that stated things like IT IS AROUND THIS TABLE WE UNDERSTAND BEST THE WARMTH OF BEING TOGETHER, and there is always a nice-smelling candle burning in the house.

Mom loves to love, a trait that has trickled down to me too. She pours herself into her friendships and her responsibilities as a mother and grandmother. When I was in third grade, I used my saved-up money to get a sticker picture from the photo booth at the Disney Store in the shopping mall. I brought the sticker home as a gift to Mom. She was so touched that I had spent my own money on her (I did learn the art of gift giving from her, after all), and she proudly placed my Winnie-the-Pooh sticker on her mirror in the bathroom so she could look at my smile every morning. Time can be cruel, especially to stickers, so the image is long gone, but there are still remnants of the sticker there today, which she refuses to wash away. Mom loved my gifts, no matter how bad they were (don't get me started on the Popsicle-stick Christmas ornaments that she still hangs to this day!). She was also an encouraging audience member. While she would be folding baskets of clothes or painting her nails at the kitchen table, I'd do my best pop diva performance on the karaoke machine in the living room, costume changes and all.

Mom and Dad were very adamant that we spend time together as a family, especially at mealtimes. If everyone was home, we ate dinner together as a family. Even if the meal was rushed because we needed to get somewhere after dinner, spending time as a family was important to my parents.

My parents also valued a strong work ethic and taught us to "earn our keep." They were also very strict about money, and whatever money we had to spend on ourselves was earned or saved from birthdays or special occasions. It always surprised me when other kids talked about getting money, or an "allowance," from their parents for no reason. My parents wanted us to learn the value and benefits of hard work from an early age. It was expected that I vacuum, dust, sweep, mop, and clean my room every day. On the weekends, Dad would typically need help in the yard or down at the barn. We could earn some spending money if we helped with extra chores beyond what was expected of us. "Why would I buy a dishwasher when I gave birth to three?" Mom always joked as she piled the dinner dishes up next to the sink and my brothers and I argued over whose turn it was.

When it came to family finances, Mom ran a tight ship. She was great at stretching a dollar and making sure we always had plenty of food on the table, and it always felt special, even if a lot of it was canned or from a box. On Christmas mornings, Mom would serve her famous home-made cinnamon rolls, a tradition that continues to this day. We would come home from evening church service on Christmas Eve, my parents would kiss us good night, and I'd fall asleep watching the snow flurries outside my window while the whirling and knocking of the old bread machine on the kitchen counter hummed me to sleep. Mom would have to get out of bed at three a.m. to roll the dough out onto the counter and cover it to let it rise once more before the sticky buns were tossed into the oven as we opened presents around the tree.

Dad had his special treats too. When I was very young, in the fall and winter, Dad often brought home meat from the buffalo packing slaughterhouse where he sometimes picked up extra hours. It was always a special night when he brought home ribs; even though he'd work late on these nights, we'd stay up waiting for him to get home and grill immediately. In the summer, we would line up along the side of the road to buy sweet corn from a well-known local farmer. You had to watch the news to see when he was available.

Mom taught me the important lesson that it's not necessarily what's on the table that matters, so much as who is sitting around it. She loved having her kids and husband gathered to share a meal, no matter if it was an expensive steak dinner or boxed macaroni and cheese. She continues to seek out meaningful time and connections with the people she loves, and taught me how a simple call or homemade batch of soup for a sick friend can go a long way.

Mom and Dad were good at making everything special, whether it was a good year for the family business or not. Money wasn't always steady, and I remember when Dad would come home with payment for some work he completed. Mom would drive up to the bank and deposit the money before we headed to my brother's baseball game or a rehearsal, because the money needed to be in the bank account the next day to cover the bills. I started to learn that our relationship with money depended on how we prioritized it as a family and how quickly or slowly we spent it.

In the years after I finished college, when I had to pay for something I didn't quite have the money for, I sometimes thought about the moments when Mom was stressed about money and how she made it all add up. I'd think about Mom, in a bathrobe, her hair still wet from the shower, getting her purse and writing me a check for school lunches, saying that it might not be enough for the entire week. Today I realize how difficult it must have been for her to express that kind of worry to her kids. Mom and Dad did a good job at hiding the hard parts about money from us. We were blessed in many ways, and my parents made sure that we expressed our gratitude and appreciation for those blessings. They never wanted me to feel bad about needing money, but I began to understand that money can be a tough subject, especially when you need to think about it every day and with every purchase.

They wanted their kids to value that hustle and for us to see how hard they were working for what we had. I didn't want to be a burden on my parents: if I needed to ask for money, I would spend a long time in my bedroom working up the courage and preparing my sales pitch as I waited for the right time to approach my parents about the upcoming field trip or the theater class that my friends were signing up for.

My parents worked hard to give their kids everything they could imagine, especially the things they didn't have when they were our age. I was lucky to come home to a clean and safe home, a warm homemade meal, my bedroom with books I loved on the shelf, and two parents who loved me very much and wanted to see me succeed.

Mom and Dad still live in the same three-bedroom, single-family house I grew up in. They bought it when Mom was nineteen and pregnant with my oldest brother, right after they married one year out of high school. My father prides himself on having the nicest lawn in the neighborhood—as a landscaper, he has carefully trimmed, pruned, mowed, and planted the finest of every plant to his liking. Not a blade of grass untouched, no tree ignored, every flowerpot expertly placed. I remember Mom spending hours outdoors with Dad, planting flowers and vegetables and arranging every decoration until it was just so.

We always had four-legged friends in the house, the first of which (in my time) was a Pekingese named Brittany. Brittany was succeeded by a black Lab named Brisco, whom Dad trained extensively. Open the front door, and Brisco would run outside, grab the newspaper from the mailbox, and bring it back into the house. Most days, the whole newspaper would make it into the house. Other days, Dad would be shouting swear words as he ran out into the snow in his slippers and underwear to pick up loose pieces of newspaper that had flown out of Brisco's mouth. Brisco followed Dad everywhere.

The backyard we grew up playing in has since been turned into Dad's large garden, where he grows his own vegetables that always find their way into Mom's signature salsa. Dad now practices making his own maple syrup, smoking his own beef jerky and sausages, and, during the holidays, crafting his own garlands with fresh greens from the Upper Peninsula as he watches TV and periodically checks on the smoke shack.

My parents run their own small landscaping business, and from the time I was about ten, I was helping out in some way. Every night, Dad would bring home the hydroseeder—a giant tanklike trailer filled with water and grass seed to spray on new lawns-to-be. My job most evenings was to go out to the driveway and spray down the hydroseeder with the garden hose as Dad asked me about my day at school. I was happy to help Dad, and even from a young age, I saw the exhaustion in his face when he came home. My dad has broken his back multiple times, but as soon as he recovered enough to lift something, he was right back to work. To this day, he continues to work long hours, in the sun, on his knees, straining his back and refusing to quit. Dad inspired a can-do, just-let-me-do-it attitude in me. For better or worse, that's come back to bite me when I overpromise or stretch myself too thin among friends, work, and responsibilities at home. Dad made it look a lot easier than it feels nowadays.

Working for the family business also included spending time with Mom in her office, stuffing, licking, sealing, addressing, and stamping what seemed like endless envelopes. These were the days before email, when invoices were delivered by the mail; the people owing money would send paper checks that we then deposited at the bank. Sometimes, however, Mom would have me send invoices on the fax machine, and sending faxes was the most boring, tedious, and time-consuming task. A fax machine is an electronic scanning device that can send and print images via a phone line, sort of like printers that can text each other. In the 1990s, it took about five minutes to connect to the telephone signal. The machine would scan a piece of paper (such as an invoice), and the phone line would carry that scanned image in the form of code to the other person's fax machine. Upon arrival, the receiving fax machine would print that image out on paper, whether the recipient wanted it or not. People still use fax machines today, but they're much, much faster and easier to use now.

In the winters, my parents operated a Christmas tree lot, where they would sell evergreen trees and wreaths. The lot was located next to a local bison farm, so families could make a big day of it: they'd come to see the Glezmans, buy a Christmas tree, pick out a wreath my mother had made, and feed the bison some hay through the fence. I was still quite young when Dad ran the lot, but I remember visiting him daily. Mom and I would bring a warm meal, and we'd sit in the camper turned office, waiting until a family came to buy a tree. Sometimes it was so cold that we'd watch the customers' cars from the windows to see whether or not they got out before we put our coats on to go greet them. There was a small heater in the camper, which is where I preferred to be. Once a family picked out their tree, my brothers would help move it and tie it onto the roof of their car, and Mom would help me count the money in the register out of the little white shack we'd decorated with Christmas lights.

There was an old, dusty radio in the corner tuned to the local Christmas music station.

Because of the landscaping business, the Christmas tree lot, and the simple fact that my family had lived in the area for a long time, we always ran into people my parents knew, especially my dad. People always had something nice to say about Terry and Sherri Glezman. They are generous, loving, hardworking people who love their friends, their community, and their work. Throughout my childhood, the Glezmans were a happy crew—always busy, always ready to help, and almost always together.

2

The Butterfly Effect

When I was in school, I didn't like recess or gym class. Now, I'm not against the *existence* of gym class or recess; they were just awkward spaces for me. And it's not because I didn't like playing games or having fun—it's because, in order to survive in those spaces, it helps to have friends, and I didn't have many at the time.

Once the school bell rang, all the kids in my class would rush outside toward the action while I'd hug the entrance to the playground or the gymnasium as if whatever was beyond the double doors would swallow me up and spit out my lonely, friendless bones. Kids would quickly get into their groups, shouting one another's names as they raced across the gym floor or field to plunge into whatever activity they had planned earlier that day. I'd stand at the edge of the sidewalk, looking out over the vast playground through my large, round glasses, wondering just where I was supposed to be. All around me, I'd see small groups of friends doing very different things: there were the kids on the basketball court laughing and joking with one another as they chased the ball up and down the court. Me? Jump for a ball? Not likely.

One time, I reluctantly joined the basketball team in fifth grade after a teacher told my parents it would be good for me. During one nightmare of a game, the coach actually put me in as our team, the Blair Bobcats, was losing a qualifying game during the All-City Boys' Basketball Championship. In a rare move, a teammate passed me the ball, and I took off dribbling like a kid who was touching a basketball for the very first time. My parents leapt from their seats in the bleachers and shouted my name with excitement as I stumbled down the court like a newborn giraffe trying to figure out how legs work. As I hobbled toward the basket, I was halted just shy of the three-point line when a kid from the opposing team—who was a full foot taller and a hundred pounds heavier than me—jumped in front of me, stopping my dribbling dead in its tracks. I fell to the floor face-first. My glasses went flying as my hands spread out like an upside-down snowman. I think the kids on both teams laughed. Worst of all, as I'd realized I was falling, I'd attempted to shoot the ball, and it couldn't have gone any farther from the net. Basketball, I decided, was not for me.

I surveyed the playground further. The group of kids

playing tag out in the field required far too much running in order to participate. Having learned nothing from the basketball incident, my parents once proposed the bright idea of me running on the track-and-field team in sixth grade. During one particularly hot and humid race, I rounded a corner and saw the multicolor flags signaling the finish line in the near distance with no other runners in sight. My head was pounding, my body was burning, and all I could do was sprint as fast as I could while focusing on the two feet below me that no longer felt connected to the rest of my body. My shoes hit the earth with such force that my legs felt like spaghetti noodles, and my vision started to go blurry. I stumbled toward the finish as I felt my chest sting and my heart pound with the exhaustion of a slightly-out-of-shape nerd trying his very best. As I crossed the finish line, I was convinced the heavens had opened and a miracle had taken place right there on the lawn of the Grand Traverse County Civic Center as I breathlessly finished in first place.

It wasn't, however, first place, as my mom embarrassingly told me—it was last. All the other kids had finished *that far* ahead of me. I squinted and looked around through my fogged-up glasses to see the other runners standing with their parents and teammates enjoying their postrace orange slices and juice boxes. I huffed toward a bush and puked my guts out. Running, I decided, was also not for me.

Our playground was vast, and I knew there had to be a corner for me somewhere. I watched as the competitive group playing four square smacked and flung the ball with all their might, sending kids hurtling toward the rough pavement in an attempt to save themselves from elimination. As I said, I wore big glasses and couldn't risk getting them broken by a flying ball. Whenever I ventured into four square territory, I usually left with a bruise or a broken lens, so I tried my best to avoid it.

There was a group of kids that hosted make-believe adventures near the fence by the baseball diamond, which bordered three tall stand-alone pine trees on top of a small hill. The shaded cove served as the castle, the haunted forest, and, occasionally, the hiding place to kiss your crush, or so legend had it. I was not getting any secret kisses from admirers back then. The baseball diamond was typically the desert, the battlefield, or, on very boring days, a baseball diamond. Make-believe was where I thrived, but the success of the adventure hinged on who was playing along that day. Sometimes the basketball boys would join in, but only if it involved saving a princess because that had to end in a kiss, and it was *always* about the kiss. I was more interested in the poisonous, crocodile-filled waters we had to cross to get to her pine tree . . . I mean, castle. I couldn't run, I couldn't play ball, and I had been shamed away from using my imagination and playing pretend by a lot of mean kids who didn't understand that being creative is actually really cool.

What made surviving the awkwardness of the playground harder was that I never really felt like I had a best friend.

Fitting into these spaces is always easier when you belong to a group, but I didn't feel that way for most of my childhood. I was a tiny kid in big glasses with a lot of energy and ideas, and most kids thought that meant I wasn't athletic or cool. I didn't get invited to many birthday parties, and I spent a lot of my time reading and going on adventures I made up in my head.

But one day, the opportunity presented itself, and what I thought made me peculiar turned me instead into the most popular kid in school—for a brief moment, at least.

As our third-grade class trickled into the classroom, a student announced, quite loudly, "Chasten's butterfly died!" Our class had been observing the butterfly life span over the last few weeks with living specimens, and one boy took it upon himself to proclaim that the very dead butterfly lying at the bottom of the net was somehow mine. All the kids went racing toward the butterfly net in the back corner of the classroom. They were gasping and looking back at me, waiting to see what I would do. I shuffled toward the net, trying to decide what to say once I arrived at the scene of my butterfly's final resting place.

Let me be clear: nobody had been assigned butterflies, but now that one was dead, it was apparently mine. I wasn't always a lemons-into-lemonade kid, but in this moment, I knew that I had a very important choice to make. I could deny ownership of this butterfly and claim that the dead insect was, in fact, somebody else's. Or I could plunge myself into a grief so spectacularly dramatic that every single student, teacher, and lunch lady at Blair Elementary School would be forced to send flowers and cards. I chose drama.

I looked down at the little butterfly in the pie tin at the bottom of the net. I glanced up at my classmates, who were waiting with bated breath. I slowly turned to them and confirmed that the butterfly was indeed mine. I solemnly accepted its death and informed my classmates that I would hold a proper funeral for *her* at recess. Did I know it was a female butterfly? No, I did not. That didn't matter. Every kid in my grade agreed to attend. It would be the event of the year, I decided! An event so impressive that I would be launched into the upper realms of popularity, where I would cement my status as a "cool kid." Could I borrow an organ from the music room? Where would we source the flowers? My mind was racing. This was my moment, and there were only a few hours to plan!

Throughout the morning, kids would stop at my desk to pay their respects to Mildred. (Was her name Mildred? I have no clue. But knowing young Chasten, it was either this or something equally remarkable.) While painting during art class, a friendly girl stopped by my table to ask if I was doing okay. I hung my head and thanked her for asking. "I'm hanging in there," I mumbled. One of the basketball players, whom I never spoke to, stopped at my lunch table and told me he was sorry for my loss and that he would be at the funeral. I had these kids wrapped around my finger so tight, the power was intoxicating.

The big event came, and as I'd suspected, everyone who was anyone arrived at the cemetery (a patch of dirt next to the sandbox) to pay their respects.

A girl in my class, Katie, brought me to her locker and offered a beautiful little box we could use to bury Mildred in. I couldn't believe how kind she was being to me. The butterfly coffin—er, box—was a very small ivory jewelry box with a delicate golden clasp. We placed Mildred in the box, dug a hole, and laid her coffin in the ground. Kids threw some dirt onto the grave as I recited a few words and thanked everyone for coming. But then, without so much as a grand finale or applause, everyone ran away and jumped back into their ball games and regularly scheduled playing. My moment was over.

Mildred's funeral fiasco seemed all but done until a few days later, when Katie's parents asked her where her grandmother's old jewelry box was.

Yikes.

Katie pulled me aside in the hallway and informed me that Mildred would need to be dug up because her parents needed the coffin back.

Rude.

Ever the event planner, I announced that there would need to be a second funeral at recess because Mildred's coffin was a fraud and, honestly, she deserved better. Alas, kids' attention spans for drama and butterfly grief are short, and only a few mourners came. Katie and I dug up the dead butterfly, took the corpse out of the jewelry box, wrapped Mildred in a Kleenex, and placed her back in the grave. Katie was mostly worried about how she was going to get all the dirt off the jewelry box before she gave it back to her parents.

With Mildred in the ground, things went back to business as usual at Blair Elementary. The living moved on and quickly forgot about the Great Butterfly Death of 1997. I, however, had discovered something new, something that would change my life forever. I had just discovered the art of acting. Better yet, I had discovered that I was pretty darn good at it.

3

Playing the Part

My hometown has a Main Street, USA kind of vibe—it's the kind of place where a nice lady on the street will notice that you look sad and invite you back to her house for a slice of pie, and it wouldn't be weird, because your mom went to elementary school with her. The town's wholesome image is backed up by its status as the cherry capital of the world, and we lean into it. Traverse City farmers produce 40 percent of the United States' annual crop of tart cherries. Just like in New York City, we ring in the New Year by dropping a ball, except, you guessed it, it's a cherry. We fly into the "Cherry Capital Airport," and we put cherry products in or on all possible foods both sweet and savory.

After my grandmother was widowed at far too young an age, she was remarried to a man named Vern. Grandpa

Vern was a US Air Force veteran turned electrician who also owned and operated his own cherry farm just outside of town. When my mom was old enough to work (sound familiar?), Vern used to make her pick cherries on a ladder and then sell them out of a van on the side of the road. She made a dollar an hour. Some of my only memories of Grandpa Vern involve sitting on the knee of his oil-stained overalls as my hands gripped the steel steering wheel of his old tractor. The engine would cough its thick, black exhaust as we drove up and around the rolling hills of the cherry orchard while cherry blossoms floated in the cool spring breeze that blew in from Grand Traverse Bay.

My first summer after high school graduation, I stayed true to my cherry roots and worked at the downtown location of Cherry Republic, the source for all things cherry in town, including cherry-flavored pop, coffee, tea, salad dressing, sausage, salsa, chocolates, queso dip (questionable), and . . . ketchup. Unfortunately, I was too young to serve the cherry wine.

It was a cheery cherry town. (Sorry, I had to.) I liked Traverse City proper, which is why I was very particular about claiming I was from there as a child. Downtown Traverse City was lined with cobblestoned streets featuring big houses with pillars and large front porches. (These were the kinds of people who handed out full-sized candy bars on Halloween.) Families like mine lived on the outskirts of town in subdivisions or on farms, where the pace was slower and the spaces were wider.

A confession: I have been misleading you a little bit, because technically, I grew up outside the city limits in a place called Chums Corner. In middle school, I'd ride the bus for close to an hour as it weaved through neighborhoods and subdivisions farther and farther away from town. Our bus stop was the last on the route. For whatever reason, some of the kids who lived close to the school would tease those of us who lived near the end of the route, in an area just outside the city called Grawn. The back-of-the-bus-bullies weren't exactly wrong, nor were they creative. If you look at a map, you'll see that Chums Corner is much closer to Grawn than to Traverse City—only a few roads away. ("Roads" is one of the standard units for measuring distance in Northern Michigan; the other is "hours.") "Have fun in Grawwwwwn," they'd say as they laughed their way off the bus.

The way "Grawn" rolled from their lips, you would think they were describing a type of mold. Even if they can't explain exactly why, kids can fixate on the most insignificant details like names or homes or how close to the city you live, which have nothing to do with *who you are*. A little tip: It's always best to ask someone to explain their question or insult when you sense it's meant to harm you. Bullies often recoil when they have to explain their meanness. Just ask, "What do you mean by that?" and give them time to explain. This usually reveals how weak or silly their point is.

I knew that being from Grawn meant something different

than being from Traverse City. To some kids, it meant something bad. Still, there was little I could do about the fact that Blair, my elementary school, was in Grawn. The city's public school system spans a large area that includes many smaller towns and communities, meaning one football stadium is shared between the three high schools in downtown Traverse City. So while sporting and community events brought people from the same school district together, it was clear who was from the different "sides of town."

I knew these insults were meant to make us feel as if we were less well off than our bullies, but the reality was that most of us were going home to a warm house, with food on the table and someone to tuck us into bed at night. We all had varying degrees of privilege and were lucky in many ways to have the things we had, even if we were made to believe we weren't as fortunate as other kids who lived in wealthier neighborhoods. Growing up, I felt a deep sense of shame when someone would make a comment about where our home was or what my parents did for work, but as I grew older, I learned that these insults were unfounded. My family was lucky in a multitude of ways, and I was fortunate to be reminded of that by two parents who made sure their children knew how hard they worked to make our situation a reality. I grew up with many privileges that some of my peers did not have, and although I was made to feel as if I was less than others by some of my peers, I was, in fact, a very fortunate kid.

Nobody likes being accused of being an outsider, and maybe this helped fuel the sense that I never belonged. I was constantly trying to fit in with conflicting groups. When kids put you down because of where you live or go to school, it's hard not to want their approval or validation. Why did it matter so much that our school was ten miles farther from downtown than another? And why did I care about those bullies' opinions of my community so much? Is it because I thought I couldn't be as tough and rugged as my family and classmates farther out in the country? Is it simply because I didn't want to be seen as different? I wanted to fit in somewhere, and I feared my "true self"—whoever that was—would fit in nowhere.

Still, this insecurity eventually resulted in a good thing for the community. In sixth grade, I joined the volleyball team and played most of the season in other, nicer gyms that featured big, intimidating school spirit murals, only to come home to our blank gym wall at Blair. I decided that something needed to change and that Blair Elementary would have just as much pride as the other schools. So, for a few months before the bell rang each morning, I would stand at the school entrance by myself, holding open a large trash bag and collecting pop cans in order to raise enough money to put up a mural on *our* gym wall. Pop cans come with a ten-cent deposit in Michigan, so after hauling trash bags full of sticky bottles and cans back to our neighborhood grocery store, I had recycled a couple hundred dollars' worth of materials.

That was enough to hire a local muralist to paint the school's mascot, the Blair Bobcat, on our gym wall. I asked the muralist to cover the wall in glittering gold and greens and blues. "Use as much color as you can," I explained. She told me we could afford two.

It was a start.

It's not like I had an army of friends encouraging me to do this, nor had the school approached me and asked for my help. (They didn't tell me no, though!) I'd decided that matters needed to be taken into my own hands. My motivation to see that mural on our gym wall probably had more to do with how I saw myself in the world than how I felt about the boring white wall in an elementary school gymnasium. I wanted to feel like I was on the cool side of town too. That longing started to change when I took pride in where I was, regardless of what people were saying about it.

In school, I felt a constant tug-of-war between where I was and where I wanted to be. There was the version of me I performed for my family, church, and classmates, and then this other version of myself that I felt blossoming inside but that dared not make an appearance until I was far, far away from Michigan. I did my best to blend in with my surroundings, even though looking at family photos and videos, there was only so much blending in I could do! (I was just naturally fabulous.)

As I neared middle school, I started to understand the difference between who I was inside and who the world expected me to be. Now I know that suppressing a major part of your identity will make it feel like nothing is enough, but at the time, I just felt uncomfortable in my own body, and my body was in Traverse City.

Everything I had learned about being different from what was expected (even when I didn't have the language for *why* I was different) told me that, when the time came, I needed to get out of here, and fast. Emotionally, I wanted to be where I didn't have to hide anything about myself. I loved my family and the few good friends I had, but in order to blend in with them, I sometimes had to pretend to be someone else, whether that was the country boy, the devout Christian, or, eventually, the straight kid. I'd lie awake in bed, staring up at the glow-in-the-dark stars I'd stuck on my ceiling, dreaming of packing a bag and slipping out in the middle of the night to catch the midnight train headed east (we didn't have trains, but a boy can dream) and moving to New York City to make it on Broadway. Maybe the musical *Annie* was a little too hopeful, but apparently, a kid can just show up in Manhattan with three bucks and make it big? Sign me up!

In my dreams, New York Chasten would be surrounded by friends who loved the authentic me who was hiding inside calculated and guarded Traverse City Chasten. I dreamt about shuffling through busy, taxicab-congested streets on my way to the theater as glistening marquees and sky-scrapers towered over me while the smell of food trucks and car exhaust filled the air. I was ready to exist somewhere that provided a sense of belonging.

I think it's common for a lot of young people to grow up wanting to get as far away as possible from wherever they grew up. But as I got older, I started seeing new sides of my hometown that I hadn't been able to comprehend or value when I was younger. I didn't appreciate its beauty until I moved to the desert for a summer after college to teach theater and came back craving fresh water. Traverse City itself has grown and progressed rapidly since I was a kid, changing in ways that still make my heart sing whenever I walk down Front Street or when I see the waves of the bay splashing ashore. There are many reasons why we chose to move our family to Michigan when our twins were born, reasons that twelve-year-old Chasten couldn't see just yet.

Starting in elementary school, I was notorious for writing, directing, and starring in a multitude of basement-staged, one-man productions. When our big family was gathered for the holidays, I would convince my cousins to perform in my plays, but while I was committed to an entire day's worth of work, they were usually willing to dedicate only about twenty minutes of their Thanksgiving to rehearsal (about the same amount of time the entire family was willing to sit on folding chairs or on top of storage bins in a damp and dark theater . . . um, basement, to watch a play written by a child). Slackers!

Once I learned there were productions for kids my age

at the Old Town Playhouse in downtown Traverse City, my parents happily enrolled me. Compared to the mountains of hockey and football gear my brothers were cramming into the minivan, theater was an after-school activity that didn't require much more than a highlighter and a pair of good tennis shoes. The Old Town Playhouse quickly became one of my favorite places to be. The studio was an environment where you were free to be yourself, with instructors or teachers who valued diversity and prioritized inclusion among a sea of theater nerds like me who were just looking for friends and a safe space to be the best kind of "weird." Many of the kids who came to theater class were, like me, looking for something away from a family or school they didn't mesh with. We liked improv games and playing pretend instead of smashing our faces into the ice or chasing a ball endlessly down a soccer field. The stakes in theater at that age weren't as high as broken bones on the football field, but auditions could be cutthroat, if I do say so myself.

Theater classes provided more than just an outlet for my overflowing amounts of energy. It was there that I met Jasper, a precocious and hilarious teenager two years older than me, whose mom often picked us up from rehearsal and took us for Slurpees at 7-Eleven or to a diner for pancakes, where we'd recount all the ins and outs of our upcoming production. On the weekends we'd see whatever PG-13 movie we could convince our parents to pay for while sneaking in candy that was much cheaper than the overpriced boxes at the theater.

My first big break on the community theater stage was in sixth grade for a local production of *The Best Christmas Pageant Ever*. This was a big deal, and everyone in my household heard me talk about it *endlessly*. The night of the auditions, a production company was also scouting kids to be in a TV commercial for a local trash and recycling company. (Listen, it wasn't the most glamorous role, but you gotta hustle to get somewhere in this business!) Not only did I get a part in the play, but about a week or so later, the producer called to let me know that I had landed the commercial gig. I was paid one hundred dollars and got to take an entire day off from school to film. I spent a week preparing my teachers for my impending stardom. "I just wanted to remind you I won't be here tomorrow. I'm filming a commercial and the director needs me on set all day," I'd say. They'd nod and tell me to have fun, but in my head, they gawked as I walked away, pulling my oversized sunglasses down onto my face, with a Starbucks cup in one hand and a mini-poodle in the other as I strode out of the classroom like a pop star about to take a private jet to Greece for the weekend.

The experience of filming in front of a camera made me feel like a movie star. I spent a full day in high-waisted jeans, riding a bike while making overly animated faces as everyday products around me morphed into the recycled materials they were made out of. The mailbox magically whooshed into plastic water bottles, and the asphalt on the road revealed itself to be a field of glass bottles. By the end of the commercial, after being influenced by all the recycling wizardry around town, my character came home to see a milk jug on top of the garbage can and, in a moment of tremendous selflessness, decided to pick it up and toss it into the recycling bin instead of sending it to the landfill. The range! The drama! Are you sweating? What a story arc.

The commercial aired on television later that year, and our family ordered pizza and gathered to see it for the first time. I sat on the carpet in front of the television, nervously fiddling with my fingers while butterflies fluttered in my stomach. I wasn't nervous onstage or in front of the camera, but was my family going to be impressed? The quick thirty-second ad aired in the middle of a game show called *Who Wants to Be a Millionaire*, with lots of giggles and applause as young Chasten made his television debut riding a bike behind a garbage truck. My family was proud, and I was showered with praise and hugs, which proved that I really did have something special. After seeing how my family responded, I turned my attention to the reaction at school the next day. You'd think appearing on television in a recycling commercial might prime me for some intense bullying, but some of the kids at school thought it was pretty cool, rushing up to me in the hallways to tell me they'd seen me on TV the night before. The athletic boys and the popular girls both thought I was pretty cool. At least for a few weeks.

The following year, I played the role of Mike Teavee in the community theater's production of *Charlie and the Chocolate Factory*. In the classic movie, Mike is obsessed with cowboys (close to home), but in our production, it was decided that he would instead be a big fan of baseball. (They don't call it acting for nothing!) During one performance, I stepped forward to deliver my line to Willy Wonka, who was twirling his cane . . . a *little* too enthusiastically. I was a few words into my monologue when WHACK! Wonka's cane smacked me on the head and everything went black.

I woke up on a couch in the greenroom (the theater kids' locker room) to my mom rubbing my arm and the stage manager asking if I was okay. Wonka had knocked me on the head so hard that I had blacked out onstage. But as they say in showbiz, "The show must go on!" and indeed it had. The actors had somehow improvised a way to run the rest of the show without Mike Teavee. "I still better get paid!" I shouted as the stage manager left the room.

Okay, I didn't actually shout that. I was thirteen and very much unpaid.

I obviously never made it to Broadway, but I loved acting. That feeling of standing under the hot, bright lights in front of an applauding audience proved to me that I had talent worth sharing with others. When the pulleys that lifted the curtain squeaked as it furled upward, my heart would patter just a little faster until the spotlights flashed on and the audience quickly hushed, leaning forward to hear the first line. When I was onstage, that armor I was starting to build up between my heart and the rest of the world simply melted away, even if just for a few short hours. I was alive up there, and inside those three walls of the stage, nothing held me back. I played a different person back home, on the bus, and in the hallways at school, but on the stage, the audience was rooting *for* me and laughing *with* me, not at me.

Theater became my sport of choice, but my access to acting was limited to the shows for young performers at the community theater and one class in middle and high school. (Which is actually rare. So many students don't even have a theater class! We've gotta fix that. Every kid deserves a shot at drama!) As other kids started to fix their sights on athletic scholarships, it became clear to me that, if acting was what I wanted to do, it was going to have to be somewhere big.

Even though I had never been to New York City, from what I could tell on TV and in musicals, dreams came true in the Big Apple. The concepts of success, love, happiness, friendship, and fame weren't found in middle-of-nowhere-America—they were *out there*. I felt out of place in my small town, and I knew there had to be something else for me, even if I wasn't always comfortable or confident enough to pursue that mysterious "something."

4

I Am Not a Cowboy

When I was in second grade, my brothers and I started raising livestock with some of our neighbors and friends as part of 4-H, a national youth organization that promotes STEM (science, technology, engineering, and math) education, civic engagement, healthy living, and (especially in our area of Northern Michigan) agriculture. Though it's well known in rural America for teaching young people how to raise farm animals, 4-H leads all kinds of in-school, summer camp, and after-school activities in urban and suburban areas too. It was a big scene where I grew up, and my parents were excited for us to get involved once we were old enough. A lot of our friends and family participated, so 4-H wasn't just another way for us to keep our hands busy; it was also a great way for my parents to socialize and spend a week with their friends at the county fair. I was a little perplexed by the idea at first (I wasn't sure farming or barns were really my thing), but once I learned that I didn't have to raise a pig but could instead raise a *cute goat*, I was sold.

Lucky was my first goat, and we became fast friends. (Until I had to sell him at auction—he then went to live on a local farm, terrorizing the farmers and other animals like the good agent of chaos he was.) Lucky was a bit of a knucklehead, but I've never met a goat interested in being dragged around by a ten-year-old in denim shorts and straw hat while a judge feels its muscle structure and asks invasive questions about its age and behavior. After successfully raising Lucky, I switched to raising dairy feeders (think of the classic black-and-white-spotted cows you'd see in a cartoon). Eventually, I worked my way up to showing steers (the much heavier, bigger cows with horns you might see on a ranch). Steers were regarded as a big-shot project at our fair. Since these massive (and sometimes aggressive) animals typically weigh about ten times a human's body weight, it takes a tough and dedicated kid to raise one. You'd buy the calf wild off a farm in August or September, when it's very young, and raise it for a year. The following summer, you'd bring your animal to the county fair to show it and eventually auction it off to a buyer who would process it for meat.

If you work hard at taming a steer, it will trust you. I spent so much time working with each animal that I could take them for walks in the woods or the field near our barn without needing a harness or rope. It was peaceful and calming to work with animals that large, especially when they depended on you. The hardest part for me, however, was trying to not get attached, knowing that a year later, your steer would be loaded up on a trailer at the fair and sent to slaughter. I knew it was a part of life, but that didn't change how I felt about participating in it. I wasn't naïve—I knew how meat got to the grocery store—but I had mixed feelings about taking part in that particular "circle of life."

You have to start training your steer and getting it to trust you right away. This usually meant that, every few nights after dinner, Dad would take us boys down to the barn and we'd each work with our animals. I'd walk slowly around the barnyard, trying to get the steer to let me come near it. Eventually, I could put a rope around its neck and walk it on my terms, not the steer's. This could take months. Calves are only about two hundred pounds when you get them, but they're still wild, so they jump and buck when you try to control them. Even if you do get a rope around its neck, you're bound to get dragged around in the dirt and kicked in the leg (or worse) if you aren't paying attention and in control. There were inevitably a lot of bruises those first few months of steer taming.

By the time the fair rolled around, the steer weighed between a thousand and fifteen hundred pounds and could be completely unmanageable (and scary!) if you hadn't been dedicated to taming it. It never failed that someone would bring their steer to the fair, only to be dragged around in the dirt by a wild animal they had never tamed. It would take multiple adults to corner the animal and get it under control. This wasn't only dangerous; it was also super embarrassing. Sometimes, animals got spooked and could be cornered while the 4-H'er regained control. Other times, a kid just didn't work with their animal enough, and they'd be forced to leave the fair if their animal was deemed too dangerous. 4-H took responsibility very seriously, and not being dedicated to your project was embarrassing for you, your 4-H club, and your parents.

I was in no way interested in being publicly humiliated in front of my family—or anyone else, for that matter—so I was very dedicated to the work. I was always a staunch rule follower in school, mostly because I didn't want to stick out. But when it came to the possibility of being crushed by a cow, I took that life-or-death hypothetical rather seriously.

While I did enjoy the fair and the learning opportunities it provided me, there were other social expectations about the kind of kid you had to be, and I became very focused on meeting those demands. Especially once I started to understand that I was more than just *different* and that this difference would start to become obvious the more I tried to hide it behind cowboy boots and star-spangled dress shirts.

Alongside the usual gossip, there were lots of rumors about fair romances. I always thought that my success would make girls pay attention if they heard that one of the Glezman boys was pretty talented when it came to 4-H. I know giant cows aren't the most exciting or attractive thing in the world—they're more cute than anything—but *winning* usually turns some heads, right? The truth was, though, that girlfriends weren't something I was interested in—a fact that I didn't dare admit to anyone. Besides, a bigger part of me cared more about showing my brothers that I was better at something than they were, but while they didn't care so much about blue ribbons and showing their steers, they *definitely* cared about girls.

In many of the circles I was in, there was a very specific type of masculinity, or manliness, that needed to be displayed in order to be seen as a "tough guy." To a lot of people in these circles (the county fair, school, youth group, church), masculinity looked only one way. Any male who displayed emotions or behaviours outside of those narrow expectations was typically regarded as less than or weaker, and often made fun of for it. While there were many pressures coming from a lot of the male-dominated circles in my life, I had a strong role model in my father. He taught me that a quiet man is no weaker than the loudest in the room, and that love and tenderness and vulnerability aren't things to be ashamed of. Now that I am an adult and very confident in who I am and what I believe, I find that those who are the brashest about masculinity or gender roles are often the most insecure about it.

Groups of these "tough guys" would roam around the

fairgrounds in their boots, dirty jeans, and cutoff shirts while picking on younger, nerdier kids like me and flirting with girls like jungle cats on the prowl. Their version of masculinity had to be exhibited in a very visible (and sometimes aggressive) way. For me, 4-H, like many other things in my early life, required a sort of performance. Cowboy Chasten (even if I was good at showing cattle) was a bit of a lie.

It was expected that country boys weren't afraid to get dirty (that part I didn't mind), but young men were also expected to be into certain things, like hunting and guns, athletics, country music, and obnoxiously large pickup trucks. These were more than activities and vehicles—they were a lifestyle. The type of truck you drove and the stickers you placed on its back window and tailgate defined you. The type of boots and shoes you wore defined you. The jacket you wore defined you. The size of the deer you killed last fall and the hockey team you played on defined you. Even the football team you cheered for defined you.

I was a lonely kid at times, and I spent a lot of time working in the barn. Sometimes this was out of necessity, like mucking the barn (the farmer's way of saying "scooping poop") or feeding the animals, but usually when I was in the barn, I just needed a quiet place to go to be away from everyone else. I liked that working in the barn meant I didn't have to worry about other people. I found a sense of calm sitting atop the barnyard gate and feeding the steers handfuls of hay. They'd stretch their necks up toward the top of the gate and stick their long, sandpaper-like tongues out and scoop the hay out of my hand while covering my jeans with long ropes of spit.

Even though I found it peaceful, it was lonely. And although I didn't see myself fitting in with most groups at school, especially the cowboys, I was still jealous that those kids *had* a group. I was still trying to find mine.

5

Cafeteria
Politics

My 4-H triumphs were not just about besting my brothers and winning gold trophies with cows on top of them. There was also a financial aspect. When your animal was sold at auction, depending on the year, you could pocket a few hundred dollars. The last year I was in 4-H, you were lucky to sell a steer for one dollar per pound. Nowadays, kids are selling their steers for close to ten dollars per pound, pocketing enough to save for college. There was no guarantee of breaking even when I was in 4-H, but in a good year, if the price of beef was high enough at auction, my savings account could see a little boost after I paid all the bills I had accumulated over the project. My parents were very strict with how we spent this money, and I was supposed to save anything left over for the next year's project and, ultimately, for my first car. Once I had saved up enough to buy a car, I could gain a little independence—so I was desperate to get a job and start earning my own money.

During summer break, my brothers worked for the family business, installing sprinkler systems and helping Dad move mounds of dirt and rock. In a classically Chasten way, I wanted to do my own thing. It was nothing against my father or his line of work; but as arguably the weakest of the bunch in terms of physical strength, I wanted to be on my own to avoid any sense of disapproval from him or my brothers. For years, I'd bothered our veterinarian about letting me work at the animal hospital. "I'm so experienced with animals!" I kept reminding everybody, but nothing came of it.

Then, one night when I was fifteen, the phone on the wall rang while we were watching TV. (Yes, you read that right—phones used to be connected to the wall with a telephone line! You would have to get up and walk across the room to answer it. Worst of all, you couldn't pause live TV, so you would miss out on whatever you were watching. I feel like a dinosaur.) Mom listened closely while the vet's office told her that they needed a kennel technician, and I could start right away if I wanted the job. It paid just above minimum wage, and I jumped at the opportunity. Since I had only my learner's permit at that time, which only allowed me to drive with a parent in the car, my brother had to drop me off at the veterinarian's after school. I'd walk all the dogs and spray down their cages, scrub the surgery areas, and clean the exam rooms after the hospital had closed. It was silent, and sometimes lonely, but it provided the perfect opportunity to work on my show tunes. When I was done, I'd call home and someone would drive down the road to pick me up and take me to the barn so I could feed the steers.

With my combined income from 4-H and the vet job, I saved enough money to buy a car: an all-wheel-drive 1992 Mitsubishi Expo LRV (you're gonna want to Google that), which an old man down the street was selling for an unbelievably low price. It had low miles on the engine, all-wheel drive for the icy winter roads, and got great gas mileage—my dad couldn't believe how good a deal it was. The only issue was that it looked like someone had smooshed a minivan into a little loaf of a car, which did not win a high school student any points for coolness. (I now drive my twins around in a plug-in hybrid minivan, and I think I'm a very cool dad.) I didn't care that other kids thought minivans were uncool—I had places to be, and the van was my ticket to independence.

I could tell that Mom and Dad were proud of my hard work and the wise choice I had made. My friends took to calling the van the Mitsushitzu (and not just because its odd shape resembled that breed of dog). The 'Shitzu was a weird car: It had only one small door in the second row on the passenger's side, and it rolled open like a van door, even though the car itself was much smaller than the average minivan. The horn was comically high-pitched, like something from a circus, which made it all the more adorable and awkward. The car just didn't make sense. I didn't take myself too seriously and embraced the funkiness, which made driving a clown car to school a little easier.

Once I had the 'Shitzu, I got a second job, busing tables at a local Mexican restaurant called La Señorita. I'd put in half my hours at the animal hospital and then run to make my dinner shift at the restaurant, stopping at the barn to feed the cows on the way. I'd put in some hours busing plates and scraping leftover burritos off the tables, and then I'd head back to the animal hospital to finish my janitorial duties. I'd get home at around ten p.m. or so, smelling like bleach and salsa.

Occasionally, my restaurant shoes were so gross that I would have to take them out to the driveway and spray off the encrusted food with the garden hose. I was known for picking up extra shifts at both jobs, and my work ethic paid off. The wait staff would tip me extra if I'd get to their tables quickly, which meant I had more gas money for the long car rides I would take on my days off. With no destination in mind, I'd spend the better part of a day driving around the hills and peninsulas of Northern Michigan with the windows down, enjoying the hot summer sun while listening to my stack of Jimmy Buffett CDs that were neatly arranged in the sun visor. To treat myself, I'd stop at McDonald's to buy a pop and some french fries. It's not like taking on extra shifts at the restaurant was keeping me from big plans with friends over the summer. I found a lot of purpose in work and knew that Mom and Dad would approve.

The 'Shitzu was a dependable car until my first semester of college, when I was driving up a hill on the way to campus and the engine just gave up with a loud *clunk*, the controls went black, and the car began to slowly fill with smoke. Thank goodness there was nobody behind me in traffic, because as soon as I realized what had happened, the 'Shitzu began rolling backward down the hill. Nervous that I was about to burst into a ball of flames, I steered the wheel as best I could as the car gained momentum. Faster and faster, the car rolled down the hill, until I was able to veer into a ditch at the bottom and come to a stop. The 'Shitzu sat there like a burnt marshmallow as I jumped out, walked away from my minivan turned fog machine, and nervously called Dad.

"Hi, Dad? I sputtered.

"Uh-oh. What's wrong?" he asked. He always knew when something was up.

"Uh, my car just blew up, I think."

"You think?"

"Okay, so it most definitely just blew up."

"Well," he said. I could hear him smiling. "That was bound to happen sooner or later."

I sold the 'Shitzu for parts and leveled up to a 2004 Saturn Ion, which was later squashed on an icy road by a beer delivery truck the day of my grandma's funeral. I'd tell the story, but I'm already embarrassed.

Winter driving is a whole different story, and around these parts; "winter" can begin as early as October and stretch until April, and during those snowy months, it's not uncommon to wake up and peek out the window to see your car covered in a foot of snow and the windshield coated in a thick layer of ice. Many of those winter mornings required running outside in my pajamas with snow up to my knees, brushing snow off the car door to get to the ignition, and starting the engine early so it could warm up and make cleaning off the pile of snow a little easier. Then I'd run back inside to finish slurping my bowl of Cinnamon Toast Crunch and throw on some jeans. Sometimes the snow was so thick, I would have to use a push broom to clear it off faster. The little brush and scraper I kept in the car were no match for a Michigan winter. As if all that stress weren't enough to start your day at six a.m., when I'd finally arrive at school, I'd be faced with the next big question: Where to park?

If you drove a pickup truck to school, you parked in the "hick" lot (a term often used to describe people who live in the country, usually used in a negative way to mean "uneducated"). Everyone understood that the hick lot was for pickup trucks, Jeeps, and the country crowd only. The folks who parked in that lot didn't think the word "hick" was insulting—they embraced it. The bigger the truck, the better. In the wintertime, it wasn't rare to see the occasional snowmobile, and in the summer, a tractor might appear. Parking in that lot meant you were as country as they come (or at least you belonged to their group), and that was a source of pride for a lot of people. Some kids were from families that had been farming in the area for generations, and other students simply found their community among those who parked there.

I'd always felt like a country boy—heck, I grew up on country music and I even liked a lot of my childhood at the barn and in 4-H—but the older I got, the more I realized I wasn't country *enough* for the kinds of folks who parked in the hick lot. By the time I was driving my minivan to high school, I knew I probably shouldn't park there. Parking, which should have been a simple task, became a bit of a political statement in high school. I was getting restless with the constant, confusing challenge of fitting in and stressing over everything I did. From the way I dressed to where I parked my van, everything was starting to feel like a bigger deal than it needed to be. Even finding a place to sit in the cafeteria was a chore. I typically floated between different groups and tables, never really having a go-to set of lunch buddies. I had my theater friends; my bookish friends who didn't say much but were happy to have company; and some acquaintances I considered more popular, with whom I would first have to make eye contact to see if it was okay to approach their table.

Fitting in is stressful and way too much work, especially when you have only twenty minutes to eat your lunch! I never really found a table that screamed *This is where you belong! Come! Be yourself!* Sometimes I would take my lunch tray into the dark, quiet hallway between the cafeteria and the auditorium. You weren't supposed to have food in there, but the theater teacher, Mrs. Bach, would look the other way if you weren't breaking any other rules. Hiding to kiss your boyfriend? Absolutely not, immediate detention. Talking on your cell phone? No way. Eating fries and reading a book? Yeah, all right, just don't get ketchup on the carpet.

With all those little pressures building up, I slowly started questioning if the expectations I was supposed to meet were meant for me in the first place. My hometown didn't offer much room for questioning the norms, and I started to feel that someone like me was going to struggle to thrive in a place where politics and attitudes favored a conservative outlook on life. I wouldn't say I was living in a bubble, exactly. I knew there were some students at school who called themselves Democrats, but I didn't really understand what made me—a Republican—different from them. Being a Republican was a political position I'd always held because the idea of questioning it (or even figuring out what it meant!) had never come up.

Until one day, it did.

In the middle of the flurry of students rushing about before the first-period bell, a friend, who eventually became one of my best friends, stormed up to me and asked why I had a political bumper sticker for President George W. Bush on my car. She had spotted it in the parking lot and wanted answers. She wondered how I could support someone like him. "I thought you would know better," she said, passing me on her way to class.

What does she mean by "someone like him"?

Like a deer caught in headlights, I stood in the middle of the morning hallway traffic feeling like an imposter. A friend had called me out for something and someone I didn't even understand. I'd just put that sticker on my car because that seemed like what everyone else was doing. My parents had those stickers on their cars. It seemed like a lot of families in 4-H supported Bush, and I thought that, as a good country boy, I was supposed to as well. Had I made a mistake? I didn't even understand what the mistake was! The truth was, I didn't know much about what made President Bush controversial. I worried that I had committed some irreversible act. Had I claimed to be someone I wasn't? Was I making a statement I didn't fully understand?

I was fifteen years old when Republican president George W. Bush ran for reelection in 2004, and I begged my parents to take me to see him when it was announced that he would be coming to our neck of the woods in Northern Michigan. I was excited that the president of the United States was going to be in my backyard! I didn't know anything about him— going to his rally was like going to see a celebrity (we didn't see many of those Up North either), rather than a politician. (To be fair to Teen Chasten, the difference is often unclear to adults, even today.)

Outside the Traverse City Civic Center, President Bush seemed to pluck the heartstrings of my fellow attendees. He spoke about the "forgotten" Americans who are taken advantage of and left with little to show for it and about the importance of a strong country full of patriotic people just like us. He made people feel like he understood their struggles. (Even though the feelings of being misunderstood and left out that I experienced weren't the same fears he was talking about. Earlier that year, President Bush had signaled support for a constitutional amendment banning marriage equality.) After his rally, with a country song called "Only in America" blasting over the loudspeakers, I grabbed one of the W stickers his campaign was handing out, and placed it on the back bumper of my car because that seemed to be the easiest way to signal to my peers, *I'm just like you. Please leave me alone.*

I don't remember thinking a lot about politics growing up, but in Northern Michigan, not thinking about politics means you likely absorb a great deal of "Being a Republican" energy and probably identify as one yourself at a young age (like I did), though you probably don't understand what that truly means (like I didn't).

I was raised Catholic, and my family was conservative in the sense that they based a lot of their values and lessons on the religious traditions they were taught as children. Our family wasn't as devout as Grandma would've wanted us to be, but we all still took the question "What would Jesus do?" rather seriously. Grandma was sensitive to us doing anything that would be shameful in the eyes of God, as if we were constantly being monitored. Religion, for me, seemed to be rooted in the fear of disapproval and punishment, rather than a belief system from which one could find purpose and enlightenment. (I have since grown to appreciate tenets from myriad religions and was even married to my husband in an Episcopal church!)

My parents didn't talk much about their personal relationship with faith or their politics at home, and it wasn't immediately clear to me the way politics as institutions and laws could have real effects on people's day-to-day lives. Politics, in a way, was distant for our family. Mom and Dad didn't consider themselves staunch Republicans or anti-Democrat; they simply felt that their concerns weren't valued by those making decisions in Washington, D.C. My parents assumed (as many Americans often do) that the people in those big white buildings in Washington didn't think or care about families like ours in rural America. Politics, however, is deeply personal. Those very personal issues we often discuss around the kitchen table—like safe neighborhoods, good schools, affordable childcare and healthcare—matter *so* much to American families. I thought politics was something that just happened on television, but looking back now, I see how policy choices were affecting my life all along.

For example, our family would occasionally load up the minivan and drive north across the channel that separated

Sault Ste. Marie, Michigan, from Sault Ste. Marie, Canada. My brother played in yearly hockey tournaments there, and while in Canada, my parents would make sure to stop by a pharmacy and pick up cheaper prescription drugs to have on hand when ear infections or pink eye would reliably rear their heads every school year. I never thought about the fact that our medicine and healthcare was more expensive in America than in Canada and that politics affected whether families could afford medicine or going to the hospital if someone got sick.

Though Mom and Dad weren't very vocal about their political beliefs, many people in some of our social circles were *very* forthcoming about theirs, most memorably when it came to people who they believed were "different." I was often perplexed by a certain friend's mom who drove us to school functions or youth group, and who considered herself a devout Christian, being bothered by any joke or roughhousing that could be perceived to be "gay." I'd wince inside when she would fire off a warning (which I'm sure she thought was a joke) about the detestable gay "lifestyle."

As I was starting to realize that I was gay, and because of the things I was learning from adults like her, I started to look inward and believe that something about me was twisted and deeply wrong. Like having bad wiring or a virus in the operating system, I wondered what was malfunctioning inside of me. The way that gay people were described by these acquaintances as "disgusting" or "evil" caused me to question God first for making me this way. *If we are all made in God's image,* I wondered, *why would he do this to me?* I didn't think to question these "friends" of my parents, since I took what adults said and believed to be the only truth available. It would take a long time on my own journey with faith to understand that I was made perfectly in the image of the God that I believe in.

Even though I knew that many young people at school or church didn't understand just how much impact their words and actions had on others (especially when it came to their blatant homophobia), the reality was that we were growing up in a bubble that made most of us feel like we had to turn out exactly how our parents or church or society wanted us to be. For me, the most common message I was absorbing in these circles was that God-fearing Americans and good country boys were tough as nails, *definitely* straight, and Republican. And good, God-fearing American country boys were the *only* kind of boys to be.

As I got older and these anti-gay messages seeped into my subconscious and took hold of my self-esteem, I realized that blending in with those around me might help me fit in and survive at school. (That's not necessarily the advice I would offer these days, but we'll get to that later!) Not only did my silent approval quickly suggest to others that I had a set of acceptable values to other people, but it also meant that I could avoid having to figure out what my values actually were. Being the right type of country boy was preapproved.

Being a Christian was expected. Being into girls and asking them on dates or to dances was the norm. If something was preapproved, then it was safe, even if it wasn't perfect. It was more important for me to protect myself than to live authentically. That's a situation that many LGBTQ+ people find themselves in. Everyone needs to be able to come out on their own terms, and in high school, I just knew that wasn't a safe option.

"But why didn't you say something?" is a question I think about a lot. The truth is, I was growing up in a system designed to keep me from questioning these norms and expectations in the first place. I didn't have the knowledge or vocabulary necessary to question or fight back against a homophobic word or symbol because I was surrounded by a straightness and religious teaching that didn't take others' perspectives, dignity, or history into account. In a community that was predominantly straight, white, Christian, and conservative, the curriculum and worldview offered up to us was a rather narrow one.

There's an expression that those who seek to build equitable groups and societies ask: "Who is at the table?" If you have a seat at the table, then you get to be part of the conversation and decision-making. You get to raise your hand and ask a question. Heck, you can even interrupt the conversation and make your voice heard if you feel like you're not being listened to. But historically, and to this day, many people are left out of important discussions about policies that will affect their own lives and experiences. These conversations can happen in your school, at city hall, or in the halls of Congress, where laws about American lives are regularly being debated and passed. Which is why it is *so* important that young people make their voices heard, even when they aren't being offered a seat at the table they're trying to access. When I was in school, the table didn't have many diverse voices present. In fact, many of those voices weren't even in the building, let alone the room!

When I was on the campaign trail, I would often meet with my team to look at the calendar and ask, "Who's missing? Who haven't we seen? Whose voice do we need to hear?" Because my experience as a gay man is only one perspective, it was important for me to hear from a variety of LGBTQ+ people who saw and experienced the world differently from me. Our community is not monolithic—that is, we are not all the same. We are a uniquely diverse community that shares vastly different lived experiences and realities. We are also an intersectional community, meaning we can share different experiences based on our heritage, race, disability, orientation, or class. It was important for me to meet with people I could learn and grow from. Not because I thought that, politically, it was the right thing to do, but because, as a prominent gay person in politics who was just given a platform, I knew I needed to make sure I was turning around and carrying as many of those voices and experiences with me as possible. If you have a seat at the table, it's important to uplift those who have yet to be heard.

When my friend stopped me in the hallway that morning in high school and called me out for signaling support for a president she thought went against my values, I had to wonder: Was I sacrificing my values to blend in with other people? And then I thought, *Wait . . . what* are *my values?* Being asked to think about my political opinions for the first time made the room begin to spin. I was laser-focused on what was in front of me and surviving high school in one piece. Now the perspective that was insulating me from many of the other big questions and harsh realities of the world was slowly starting to crack. Even though I was being challenged, I was also being invited to think and to question where I saw myself in the world. My friend cared enough to show me that perhaps I wasn't seeing the full picture, which ultimately helped me to broaden my perspective.

I wonder what it would have been like for me, being able to sit at a lunch table full of kids who didn't mind that I was gay. What if I could've stopped spending so much energy on hiding and instead had more time to focus on my passions and my academics? Better yet, what would it have been like to be surrounded by people who were experiencing life in the same way I was?

This is why it is so important to go out of your way to make sure that everyone feels welcome and accepted for who they are. You never know everything your peers are going through, and sometimes all someone needs is a safe and welcoming place to eat lunch. Even if you'll never be best friends with everyone around you, we can all at least make sure each person feels valued as a human being and welcome to share a lunch table when they just want to eat some pizza and finish their algebra homework.

I had an inkling that maybe there were other kids "like me" in high school, but it was just a vague sense that perhaps a friend and I shared a secret. Maybe—even though we never spoke of it—we could've connected over the feeling of not fitting in or of existing in an environment that told us to hide our true selves. What I do remember, most vividly, were the put-downs, the fear, and words like "fag" and "faggot" and phrases like "mama's boy"—descriptors for boys who were feminine, soft, and weak—being tossed around on the bus or in the hallways. Kids would react to something they thought was bad or uncool with the expression "That's so gay."

Bullying turned more physical in middle school, and getting pushed into a locker while getting called a "freak" by insecure boys who had more anger than they knew what to do with became more routine. Sometimes people made comments about people's presumed identity that I found to be much more hurtful than being called a "freak." One student in our grade, who I don't believe was out at the time, seemed to be the butt of some very ignorant and specific jokes about their presumed gayness. Rather than speak up, I crouched down lower, afraid of intercepting any of the harsh blows myself. I wish I'd had the strength and confidence to say something. And yet, it shouldn't be the burden of the outcast alone to speak up. Why wasn't anyone else standing up for them? Why did it need to be the other gay kid? They (we!) needed allies, and I didn't see many coming forward.

"You're different" is a pretty common excuse for kids to pick on one another. Yeah, so what? We're all different. That's a good thing! But hearing "You're not a real man" or "God hates you" hurt me much worse. Something in those insults suggested that other kids knew more about me than I did myself, and I didn't like it. I especially resented not being able to change the thing they didn't like in the first place.

I know we were all just trying to find our place, swimming in an ocean of hormones and loneliness and confusion. Fighting the waves of exclusion, I often felt like an undertow was pulling me away from everyone and everything. That undertow can have its grip on a lot of us, and many people struggle to figure out who they are or what they believe in during their childhood and adolescence. Oftentimes, those who feel lost will express their confusion and pain by taunting and bullying others who are just as lost as they are. When someone already feels low and alone, tearing down others can feel like a step up. I think about the girl who always made fun of me with her friends from the back of the bus, calling me my brothers' "sister." It was so pathetic—at least come up with a better joke than that!—but, at the time, it really hurt. What was causing her so much pain that she needed to pick on a kid five years younger than her? But even though kids might be confused or hurting, that doesn't mean their bad behavior is okay. Considering their situation helps us understand what other people might be going through, but it doesn't give a bully a free pass. Hurt is hurt, even if it's being done by someone who is hurting.

I wish it had been more "socially acceptable" to be gay when I was in high school. That is to say, I wish people hadn't cared about someone else's identity so much so that I had to spend every waking moment hiding who *I* was because of how *they* felt. We still haven't reached a place where everyone can feel safe, but it is slowly getting a little easier—I know that a book like this wouldn't have been published when I was in middle school! In fact, as we speak, books like this are still being banned in certain corners of this country. We've got a long way to go, but *you*, the reader, get to be a part of that promising future. In fact, when I returned to speak at my high school on the campaign trail, I was introduced to its club for LGBTQ+ students and their allies. I was floored by how warm the reception was in the same school that I had felt I needed to run from just sixteen years earlier. Change is happening, even if it's not as fast as we want it to be.

6

Bowling with the Punches

Just like in the movies, it was the hormones of middle school that made the world of this closeted and confused gay kid come alive. One minute I was walking to German class, and the next thing I knew, a handsome guy would walk past me in the hallway and I'd have to scoop my jaw up off the bubble-gum–laden floor. I felt like I was experiencing the first symptoms of a chronic illness, and for all I knew, that just wasn't normal or right. I never considered "being gay" as a simple and straightforward explanation for what I was feeling—and one that carried about as much weight as having brown hair or glasses. Between everything I'd heard and the feelings I was coming to terms with, being gay was starting to feel like a giant, oozing pimple on my forehead: glaringly obvious, but, for society's sake, necessary to hide from everyone else.

"Being gay is bad" was all I knew to be true, and because of that, I couldn't pause, assess these new feelings for the cute guy wearing the hoodie in the back of class, and think, *Oh, I'm gay. Moving on!* Instead, I turned inward and started trying to find ways to stop this feeling from happening. It is heartbreaking to think of how much pain my younger self felt at the prospect of being around other students in my grade. But my terror, mixed with a sense of deep shame, made me dread being around them, especially in gym class. When it came to the locker room, I'd just reapply deodorant, wipe my face, and rush out of there as fast as possible.

Not being out in school felt like an open wound that just wouldn't heal. The taunts and bullying started to sting worse the older I got. As the truth grew clearer and clearer, I pushed it deeper and deeper into the closet. By high school it felt as if my heart were on the outside of my chest: exposed, vulnerable, and easy to break. It didn't take much to hurt me, like the day a group of seniors surrounded me and started taunting me. Out came the insults and accusations. "You like what you see, faggot?" "Stop staring at me, faggot." They egged each other on while I quickly gathered my things, desperately looking for a gap between two of them that I could escape through. I pushed my way out of their circle while they high-fived one another in fits of laughter. Not stopping to look up at anyone, I made my way to the auditorium instead of heading to math class.

Mrs. Bach never asked questions when I'd show up during a class period that wasn't mine and shuffle up to the seats at the far back of the theater. Fighting tears that were begging to be let loose, I watched the class on the stage below until my heartbeat eventually slowed and my breathing returned to normal. Wiping my tears, I'd go back to class and pretend like nothing had happened. At the time, I didn't think the principal's office was the right place to go for being called homophobic slurs. I wasn't confident that the principal cared, nor did I want to be outed to my parents by him. For all I knew, the main office wasn't a safe space for a kid like me.

That wouldn't be the last time those bullies would gang up on me. Once, on my way out of the locker room, a group of them started pushing and pulling me around by my backpack. Before I knew it, I was on the ground. I lay there, eyes squinting while studying the patterns of the vinyl tiled floor, waiting for the next blow. My brother happened to be walking down the hallway at the same time, saw what was happening, and got them to leave me alone. I knew my brother loved me and wanted to protect me, but I could see on his face that this was embarrassing for him, too. Once the bullies dispersed, he walked away, and we never said a word to each other about it. When we sat around the dinner table later that night, we pretended as if nothing had happened. I can only imagine what those guys said to him later. I didn't want to be what they were calling me, and I'm sure my brother didn't want to be related to one either.

One of the worst feelings in those rough days was the isolation—not knowing who I could run to or what I could say. Even though Mrs. Bach made the theater a place where I felt safe, I never had the courage to open up to her about all my fears and conflicting thoughts.

While my peers likely had the same amount of exposure to out-of-the-closet gay people that I had (i.e., basically none), the way they talked about gay people as if they were swamp creatures made me even more fearful of both myself and what could happen to me if they discovered the secret I was hiding. The message wasn't just: *Gay men are swamp creatures.* It was more like: *Gay men are swamp creatures . . . who should be attacked.* Alongside all the hate, a gay person was often thought of in extremes, as either victim or prey. If a gay person was in the news, it was likely about how they'd been harassed, bullied, beaten up, or worse.

The handful of anti-gay horror stories I saw in the news traumatized me, but I was especially affected when I learned about what happened to Matthew Shepard, a gay college student who was brutally murdered in Laramie, Wyoming, in 1998. Shepard had met two men at a local bar who'd convinced him to go for a ride in their truck. They took him to a remote area of town, tied him to a fence, robbed him, took his shoes, beat him in the face with a handgun, and left him to die in the bitter cold. His parents recognized him only by his braces. Matthew's murderers tried to argue in court that they panicked when they thought he was flirting with them.

This is often called the "gay panic" defense, which is still successfully used by lawyers in some states today as justification for committing hate crimes against LGBTQ+ people, especially trans people. Defendants will argue that they were scared and therefore "panicked" when they killed or hurt someone simply because they found out or even *suspected* that the victim wasn't straight. Believe it or not, sometimes the judge or jury will believe the defendant, and charges will be dismissed or the punishment will be adjusted. The judge in Matt's case didn't allow that defense to stand.

At Matthew's funeral and at the trial for his two murderers, members of what is now a well-known hate group, the Westboro Baptist Church, showed up to protest with signs that read GOD HATES FAGS and MATT IN HELL. This was exactly the kind of hate I feared some Christians would hurl at me if anyone found out about me. (Christian extremists eventually did come to protest me and my husband on the campaign trail, but by then, I had become untouchably confident in who I was, so their words were nothing but background noise.) Matthew's murder was probably the most publicized gay-hate crime of the decade, and it hit way too close to home for me—like it could happen to someone like me in "flyover country." I had nightmares about Matthew Shepard's murder. As a result, I never even contemplated suggesting that I was gay—or even brought up the subject of anyone *else* being gay—even to people I trusted for a long time. Would my friends, family, neighbors, and schoolmates turn on me, or worse? I didn't want to find out.

I now understand that this is how homophobia works: when people are scared or feel threatened, they puff themselves up to make what's threatening them feel small. At the time, it worked on me. I felt like I was some kind of unknown *thing* whose characteristics were so freakish that they were difficult for even me to understand. I now know that there were other closeted gay people around me, in school and in Traverse City. But they must have felt the same way that I did: unsafe, afraid, alone, unnatural, and ashamed. My friend Luke, who was on the bowling team with me, also came out after high school. We never discussed being gay until much later in life, but in high school, we identified with each other. We knew without speaking about it that we were two outcasts who didn't blend in very well. Even when we'd get together with friends to play Nintendo or sing along to musicals, not a word was said. Ever.

If I couldn't address what was burning inside me, I knew I needed to focus on an exit strategy. If I was going to survive this *thing*, I needed to get out of Traverse City. So, how was I going to make that happen? There was a lot of pressure in school and in my town to hurry up and achieve the *insert the sounds of angels singing* *Amerrrrrrrican Dream*. The "American Dream" was sold to my generation (and many, many that came before) as *the* definition of patriotism and success. We had all been taught that, if you worked hard, you could make good money, get (straight) married, buy a house with a white picket fence and trampoline, drive a big truck, put food on the table, and raise your 2.5 kids the way the Good Lord and George Washington intended. Never mind that there are a lot of factors that change this reality for millions of Americans, such as where you grow up, generational wealth, access to education and opportunity, your race, disability, gender, and more. I was beginning to realize that no matter how hard I worked, I was never going to be less gay, but it seemed possible that I could get smarter and achieve more if I put my mind to it. This isn't uncommon for LGBTQ+ people.

Being gay did not feel like something I could get out of. In fact, it was starting to feel like the thing that was going to *prevent* me from achieving anything at all—that is, if anyone found out. So I stayed focused on blending in and working my way up. If I couldn't shake this, then I was going to outwork, outshine, and outperform everyone else.

My awkward sense of style reflected my desperation to be a part of something solid and defined. Deep in my heart, I knew I'd never come close to looking like the popular jocks and the "in crowd." I could barely walk through the mall without feeling like a total fraud when I passed the stores where the cool kids shopped. I remember begging my mom to let me shop at American Eagle or Abercrombie, because those were the brands all the cool kids wore, but the clothes were much more expensive than what we could find elsewhere. A jacket that *looked* like a North Face fleece (but wasn't) would save my parents tons of money, but every kid wanted the real deal because the cool, rich crowd could tell the difference. (The look was to wear a hoodie underneath a North Face jacket. Remember, this was Northern Michigan—we had to dress warm to look cool.) I knew Mom felt a lot of pressure to give us what we asked for, but the truth was, unnecessary luxuries weren't reasonable, and paying hundreds of dollars more just for a tag with a certain name on it was silly. Kids are always going to judge one another at school, especially on their appearances, and Mom knew that a coat, and not a brand, was what was going to keep her kid warm.

Still, I was usually shocked at how good Mom was at finding deals. She prided herself on snagging a discount over a name brand. Every year before school began, Mom would take us to an outlet mall a few hours away from home and let us pick out some new shirts and essentials for school. We could save a lot of money this way, and anything beyond what Mom was willing to spend on school supplies had to come out of our savings. I remember buying a shirt from Hollister and wearing it obsessively. These things felt like absolutes growing up. "Do or die," as they say. If we didn't do it, then the whole world would fall apart, especially because we assumed everyone cared about it so much. *If I don't wear American Eagle jeans, nobody will think I'm cool, and then I won't make friends, and then I'll drop out of school in embarrassment and never go to college or have a good job or marry a handsome prince!*

It's going to be okay, I promise.

Learning to stop comparing ourselves to others is a life-long journey, but one that gets much easier the moment our worth isn't tied up in what others are wearing or doing. It took me a long time to learn that the opinions of others only matter if I choose to let them. I didn't need to take advice from people I would never ordinarily ask for advice. I'm reminded of one of the best nuggets of wisdom I was given growing up: stop trying to be liked by everybody. You don't even like everybody! I think I was lucky that I didn't have access to the kind of social media we have today (Facebook had just started to become a thing when I was in high school), because as a teacher, I saw how these platforms were slowly seeping into everything my students were obsessing about, and that worried me.

Our world can feel overly connected these days, and with apps like TikTok, Twitter, Snapchat, and Instagram, there are so many ways to find community with people all around the world, especially those with shared interests. I often advised my students to "pay attention to what you pay attention to." That is, be aware of where you're invest-ing your energy and attention. The internet and social media tend to suck us into a black hole where time loses all meaning. Have you ever found yourself doomscrolling? Just mindlessly scrolling and scrolling through content that overwhelms, exhausts, and bums you out? It's hard to pull away from content that fires you up. Like videos of politicians or talking heads debating your fundamental rights, or seeing article after article sounding the alarm on global warming, corporate greed, and gun violence. It's completely overwhelming and difficult to process. How many times have you been watching YouTube videos while simultaneously DMing to your best friend TikToks that have found their way onto Instagram? (I sure have.) There's a tornado of content out there that is always ready to scoop you up and whirl you around until you click the power button and come back down to Earth. It's really important to be kind to yourself when you're on these platforms—it is *so* easy to get wrapped up in what other people think and do, to the point where we can start to lose a sense of our own values and even our sense of self. Sometimes social media isn't always a conversation, so much as it is a lot of people yelling into the void, hoping someone will notice.

It's easy to get drawn into a cycle of comparison when it feels like we have an up close and personal view of everyone's life. We can feel totally isolated in our homes, schools, and small communities, but then we go online or look at our phones to see other people interested in the same things as us, and we feel a little less alone. Social media can be a game changer for inclusion and community building, but it is also a slippery slope and can easily trick us into comparing ourselves to others. There's a fine line between connection and comparison, and since we never really know what someone else is going through, we can never be sure if what we're seeing online is the authentic—or at least complete—version of someone.

I sometimes ask myself why I follow certain accounts, and I try to check in every now and then to answer the question: Is this helping or hurting? (There are a lot of parenting, news, and fitness accounts that actually cause me stress! I don't need to be *that* connected.)

Social media is always there, 24/7, ready to make you feel just a little more inadequate, worried, and perhaps a little more suspicious of your own worth if you don't regulate how much time you spend in that bubble. Be careful with this. You're only "weird" or "inadequate" if you decide you are. You are worthy when you tell yourself you are. If you use these online tools wisely, they can be a great way to feel seen and to connect with your friends, family, and the wider world.

Anyways, I'll get off my soapbox! I can hear my middle school students groaning in the back of my mind. Am I becoming too much of a dad already? I won't apologize!

I was so absorbed with making sure I looked "normal" (straight and trendy) in high school that I would put on an outfit, go to the bathroom, look in the mirror, return to my room, and try another option. My brothers would poke fun at me for changing outfits so often that I would sometimes take multiple choices to the bathroom so they didn't see me walking down the hallway as much. They were well-known athletic jocks, so simple jeans and a hoodie was cool for them. The more popular a person, the less they had to worry about impressing anyone. They were already impressive.

Once, during a school spirit week, the class council sold purple T-shirts, and because of the ridiculous gender stereotypes I'd grown up hearing (purple was a "girl color"), I was afraid that wearing the shirt would give away my big secret. So I just didn't wear one. (By the time I got married, though, that had changed—purple was one of our wedding colors.) The idea that people need to *look* a certain way is bologna sandwiches; we need to stop putting so much pressure on one another to dress or present a certain way. Fashion is fun and a great way to show your creativity and personality, but exclusion in the name of fashion is where we need to draw the line.

Despite all the confusion and silly expectations of high school, I wasn't a *total* loner or outcast. I had a varied group of friends, a few people I was very close to, and more whom I didn't become close with until after college, when we could focus on what we really needed or wanted out of friendships. Most of my friends in high school came from what you might call my "eccentric" extracurricular activities. Along with the people I met in community theater, I had made some friends from the bowling team. Yes, my school had a bowling team, and, yes, I was on it. *Very* on it. I was highly competitive, bowling up to six days a week. I was also in a recreational bowling league that met on Saturday mornings, which gave me more time to hone my skills. After high school, when I was living at home and attending the local community college, I bowled in a league with my parents. They were there to have fun, but *I* was there to win. Bowling with your parents was already funny to some people, so if I was going to be *that* guy, I was going to be a winner. Young Chasten took bowling very, very, (deep inhale) *very* seriously. (Exhale.)

Another core group of friends belonged to a program called Odyssey of the Mind—OM, for short—which was essentially a creative problem-solving competition that blended many technical and performance elements of theater, forensics, and robotics. Each team had to devise an eight-minute skit that would satisfy a list of requirements. Our team would choose a problem in the fall and have until spring to write the skit, make the costumes, build the set, and perfect the scorecard to ensure we could be awarded the maximum number of points in each category. An essential element of OM was that it was completely student driven, which meant that parents and coaches weren't "allowed" to help in the construction or writing. (You could always tell when *those* schools rolled into competition. No way those ten-year-olds had built that set! And, no, I'm *not* bitter.)

One year, an element of our problem required our main character, the hero of the story, to communicate with animals and help them in some way. So we wrote a skit about a hero with the ability to talk to birds through song. While trekking through the forest, he and his goofy sidekick (enter Chasten in a costume made of beach towels) stumbled upon a bird living in captivity (a cage made of straws and cardboard) and had to fend off the bird's captor (a woman determined to collect the feathers of rare birds for her elaborate outfits, which were actually constructed from material off the clearance rack at Jo-Ann Fabrics). Then our hero and his buddy celebrated the rescue of this rare bird with a dance (a slightly exaggerated description of what we actually did in front of the judges). In the end, we rocked it. We had done this all on our own, and we were so proud of our accomplishments. Each time we won, we wore those medals around our necks the next Monday at school, just like when the soccer or football team came home with a new title. On the morning announcements, the front office would declare that the OM team had placed first in Regionals or second at State Finals, and out of the ten people clapping in the entire school of nearly two thousand people, we'd be five of them.

My teams were always pretty good, and during my junior year, we even made it all the way to World Finals! . . . Which was held in Ames, Iowa. During our tense performance that year, when it came time to perform the celebratory dance, I ran behind the background we had constructed out of plywood to hit play on the stereo.

I hit play. Nothing happened.

I smacked the unit and hit play again. Nothing happened.

We only had eight minutes. If you went over time, you were penalized, and at World Finals, every fraction of a point mattered. I hit play again, and still nothing happened. I didn't have time to figure out the connection to the stereo or why the music wasn't playing—we had this routine rehearsed down to the second. I ran back around the set and looked up into the auditorium to see my mom and coach watching nervously, staring back at me with facial expressions that only meant one thing: *Do something!*

So I just started singing. (It is important to note that I cannot sing . . . well.) The rest of the team looked at me as if I were yodeling "All I Want for Christmas Is You" with my pants around my ankles in front of the judges. I grinned as wide as I could while singing our song, indicating that, yes, something was very wrong and, unfortunately, this is what we were doing now. And, yes, I know we're at World Finals, and, yes, I know this means we're probably going to lose, and, yes, I know that we're in front of all these strangers in Iowa pretending to be knights who wear Birkenstocks and have swords made out of toilet paper tubes, but HELP ME OUT HERE!

Out of thirty-five teams, we placed fourteenth. (While researching this book, I discovered that all the World Finals scores are still available online. I have to say, I remembered us doing a lot better, awkward dance and all.) Even though we didn't win, my mom was very proud. The fact that she must have realized how *different* I was from her other sons

while watching me be my absolute goofiest and most creative self in these competitions isn't lost on me now. There I
was, in tights and a costume made of old bath towels, winning medals for singing, dancing, and jumping around in a
feather boa, while my brothers were winning trophies for
weight lifting and football.

Most of the kids from our team went home early to
attend junior prom. I stayed in Iowa for the awards cere-
mony. I knew we weren't going to win, but I felt more at
home there than I would have in the dimly lit gymnasium at
my high school. Though some people would consider missing prom to be a crushing disappointment, I didn't mind at
all. A few weeks before World Finals, I'd had to let my date
know I couldn't make it to the dance anymore (my date was
a girl, so, uh, I wasn't necessarily thrilled to be going in the
first place) and was content to spend more time with my
drama teacher, my mom, and other OM competitors from all
over the world. I was getting a glimpse of what my creativity
could do for me in the wider world.

Now a part of me does wish I'd experienced prom—that
I had gotten to dress up, watch my date awkwardly fumble
with a boutonniere until someone's mom had to step in to
pin it on me instead, and dance with my classmates as a
chocolate fountain burbled in the background. In fact, I never
went to my senior prom, either. But ultimately, I'm okay
with it, because I wouldn't have been able to go as myself. I
belonged in the arena with the other geeks.

Looking back on it, I probably would have felt out of place even if I weren't gay: I was a farmer/actor/nerd you might have recognized from the Christmas tree farm or the recycling commercial, who could often be spotted wearing Hawaiian shirts while driving his fifteen-year-old minivan to his job as a busboy at the Mexican restaurant. I was clearly a little "different" in a town like Traverse City. Besides bowling, Odyssey of the Mind, and theater, I could be found at home reading, organizing my extensive flag collection, or down at the barn taking care of the animals.

Once I started working, my schedule was packed enough that I didn't have much time to feel lonely or out of place. But I don't remember a lot of joyful high school experiences with my peers—mostly isolation. Once, during Thanksgiving break when I was in college, I met up with some former classmates I'd gotten close with after graduation. Gathered around a table sharing our memories from high school, I realized I didn't have much to offer by way of memorable nights and bad dates. I listened as they reminisced about stuff I'd thought only happened in movies: times when their parents had gone out of town so they'd thrown huge parties, going to Florida on spring break with a bunch of friends, or that time they drove out to Lake Michigan and had a big bonfire. All I could think was that I could have never imagined doing those kinds of things in high school. I couldn't even believe that other people had done them. How did I not see (or get invited to) any of this? The nights

I remembered most entailed double features at the movies, playing video games at Luke's or Jasper's house, or staying home alone, when I would close my bedroom door, climb into bed early, and just stare out the window at the bright Northern Michigan stars, dreaming of an escape, wondering what, if anything, was in store for me.

There were a lot of lessons I needed to learn about myself and my worldview after high school, some of which required leaving the bubble I'd spent my entire life in. I needed to be able to examine my upbringing and sense of self from the outside, so I started looking for ways to burst that bubble and climb out of it.

7

How Do You Say "I Think I'm Gay" in German?

It was a seemingly normal day in Frau LaBonte's junior-year German class when an opportunity to emerge from the bubble of Northern Michigan presented itself. (I had been studying German since the seventh grade, as it was well known that the jocks took Spanish, the sophisticated and popular kids studied French, and the geeks ended up with German.) Frau LaBonte was attempting to get through her end-of-class announcements as the bell rang and students loudly packed up their belongings. In her hand was a flyer for the Congress-Bundestag Youth Exchange (CBYX) program. Moving against the sea of students heading toward the door, I listened to her explain that this particular program was an all-expenses-paid scholarship to study abroad in Germany for a year. A one-way ticket out of Traverse City?

A year abroad and the end of my stint at this high school? The opportunity to travel, make new friends, and see a part of the world I had only dreamt of? An impressive anecdote for my college applications? This opportunity was checking every possible box I could think of!

Now I just had to figure out how to get it.

CBYX is a joint effort between the American and German governments that sends a group of American high school students to spend a year abroad in Germany, attend a German high school, and live with a local host family. Overseen by the US Department of State, Congress-Bundestag students serve as "citizen ambassadors" who "represent the spirit, values, and diversity of the United States."

When it came to spirit, I had a lot of it—jazz hands and all. Diversity? Well, yes, but, uh, not in a public way. I wondered: Was I worthy of representing the United States? If I were selected, what would that say about me? Was I a model American?

When I asked Frau LaBonte to clarify that the program was a scholarship and that the year abroad was *free*, she confirmed that it was while reminding me that getting the scholarship was a *really big deal*. As she handed me the flyer, she looked me in the eye and said, "I really think you should consider applying, Chasten. This would be great for you." For once, I felt that an adult was taking me seriously and pushing me to consider what I wanted for myself. I was a hardworking and dedicated student with a report card that reflected it (well, mostly—ugh, math). I didn't have to stay in this small town forever if I didn't want to. Now a teacher was pushing me to the edge of the diving board of possibilities. I just had to decide if I wanted to jump.

I took the flyer and immediately began preparing the sales pitch for my parents.

As the dinner table conversation came to a lull that night, I mentioned that my German teacher thought I was a great fit for a study-abroad program next year and that, wouldn't ya know it, it was free! A single eyebrow was raised; they were skeptical. Mom and Dad listened as I nervously presented my résumé of hard work, good grades, and responsibility as if I were applying for a bank loan. They were probably worried it *would* end up costing a lot of money somehow, but they also thought that a year abroad might be dangerous. How was a seventeen-year-old supposed to survive on their own, halfway across the planet? Neither of my parents had traveled overseas before, and my mom didn't want her "baby" to be gone for a year, especially his senior year, which was a very big deal to her.

I had a great relationship with my parents in high school, and I assumed they saw my desire to leave as a sort of betrayal or a rejection of what they had worked so hard to build for me at home. My parents had lived in Traverse City all their lives. Many of my friends were first-generation college students, the first in their families to leave Traverse City and go to college. Leaving home was considered a little suspect, suggesting you thought you were "too good" for everyone else, even though it felt like most students in my grade were planning to leave in one way or another. Everything you could ever possibly want or need was right in our backyard here in Northern Michigan. You were supposed to be grateful for what you had, especially your family. My family was an entire world of its own. If I had one eye on a different, "wider" world, what would that say about them?

Many parents in my generation didn't have the chance to go to college or simply didn't need college degrees to have a successful career, including my father, who successfully started a family business without attending college. For my generation, however, a college degree was almost mandatory, and the goalpost just keeps getting moved. When I worked at Starbucks after college, all my coworkers had a bachelor's degree, and many of them were working that nine-dollars-an-hour job while enrolled in graduate school. It was hard to get ahead without a college degree when everyone applying for entry-level jobs had more qualifications on paper.

I dreamt about Germany for weeks. While sitting in class, I'd stare out the window and watch the airplanes flying overhead, wondering where they were going. The sun would beam in through the tiny windows that lined our classroom as I leaned on my hand and daydreamed. I'd imagine myself on one of those big airplanes, headed across the ocean for the very first time. I'd arrive in a new place, instantly make friends, and, most importantly, begin life anew in a place where I would finally fit in. Germany seemed like too good an opportunity to pass up, so, in what might have been my first real act of rebellion, I forged my dad's signature on the application and waited, holding my breath every time I opened the mailbox.

Faking my dad's signature was highly unusual. I did *not* disobey my parents, but I wanted this *so* bad. I feared Traverse City was going to swallow me up if I didn't make a move. When Mom and Dad said to call home at 9:00 p.m., I called at 8:50. If they said to be home at 11:00 p.m. and I pulled into the driveway at 11:10, I would apologize profusely the moment we made eye contact. I had seen enough of the aftermath of their "disagreements" with my brothers to know exactly how much trouble I would be in if I broke the rules. When we were young, we lost the Nintendo. When we were in high school, we lost our driving privileges, meaning no fun on the weekends. I couldn't stomach the loss of my Saturday-morning bowling league.

But I didn't feel like I was *really* breaking rules when I sent in the application. I just wanted to apply as an experiment, to see if the program would even take someone like me. On paper, I didn't seem like the outcast I felt I was in school; part of me was testing the waters to see if I'd seem like a weirdo to a panel of strangers who were trying to determine if I had what it took to represent my country well.

What was the worst that could happen if I got accepted? I'd have to tell my parents what I'd done, but their disappointment would be balanced out with pride. Only one hundred kids got to go each year!

Soon enough, I got a letter from the program inviting me for an interview, so it was time to tell my parents the truth. I decided to play it cool and ignore the fact that this opportunity was a result of my own actions. "Hey, Mom and Dad, the German program invited me for an interview— isn't that great?" Mom was very skeptical, and I think a little heartbroken, because, as she later told me, she knew I would probably be accepted. I had good grades, I had studied German for years, and I think she understood that, although I didn't fit in at school, I was well suited for this type of program, which required independence and responsibility. I was very familiar with those traits, but always with the knowledge that my parents were there to catch me should I fall. Mom knew I wanted to leave the nest—the nest she had worked so hard to build for me, and the safety net I could fall back onto when things got too hard. If I went to Germany, that net wouldn't be there to catch me, and I'd have a lot to figure out on my own. She didn't like the idea of not being there to protect me anymore. (I understand so many of my parents' worries now that I am a parent. As a kid, they sometimes felt annoying and overbearing. Now that I am the dad, I'm scared to walk away from my kids for two seconds. You really do wear your heart on your sleeve as a parent, and now I know Mom and Dad weren't trying to ruin a good opportunity or hold me back from having fun—they were just so scared to let me go.)

A few weeks after my interview, I got a letter from the program, letting me know I had been wait-listed. When I called to find out exactly what that meant, they told me that I hadn't been selected, but my name was on a list of kids to whom they would offer a spot if any of the accepted students dropped out. As soon as they started explaining it to me, I was crushed. I knew no one would ever drop out, especially kids like me who couldn't otherwise afford to study overseas and were now essentially being handed an escape from their small towns. But I couldn't give up hope so easily—I felt in my bones that something was going to happen. So I came home from school each day and immediately checked the mailbox, and then I'd run inside and look for a blinking red light on the answering machine that meant someone had left a voice message.

Beeeeeeeeep.

Grandma was calling to see if Mom wanted to go to bingo on Sunday. "Just call me back, love you all!" Yeah, yeah, yeah, Grandma, hurry up!

Beeeeeeeeep. Next message.

Dad's voice. "Hello? Is anyone home? Sherri? Are you there? Just calling to see if anyone is there. Okay. See you later, love you, bye." Didn't he know we were all at school?!

Beeeeeeeeep. Next message.

The prescription was ready to be picked up from the pharmacy.

Beeeeeeeeep.

"You have no other messages."

Each day, I'd go through the same motions, hoping *the* message would finally reach me. *Pack your bags, Chasten, it's your turn.*

A few months of this agony passed, and then one day, my parents were waiting for me in the living room when I came home from school. I sat down at Mom's request, and she handed me an envelope. This was unusual. It was quiet, and there was an awkward tension in the air, as if a group of people were about to jump out from behind the furniture and shout "Surprise!" but in the most somber manner possible.

"What's this?" I said, smiling as I nervously opened the card. It wasn't my birthday, so I knew something was up. Inside the card, a very heartfelt message in Mom's handwriting explained how proud my parents were of me . . . and how sorely I was going to be *missed*.

Wait a minute.

I looked up from the card and saw tears already rolling down Mom's face. Dad was smirking. "Did I . . . get it? Am I . . . going?" I asked. Mom couldn't hold back any longer. "Yeah," she said, crying, trying to play off her sadness and fear as tears of pride and excitement. The program had called her earlier that day to let her know that a student had dropped out and that I'd been selected to receive the scholarship. My parents looked at me as I sat frozen on the couch. If I wanted to go, they were okay with it. Mom hugged me, wiped her tears, and retreated to the kitchen to make dinner.

For all the dreaming I had done about running away from school, a sense of guilt started creeping in once I realized how much Mom and Dad were going to miss me. The reason I got this scholarship was thanks to them, too. They'd always pushed me to work harder and want more. They'd maintained high standards and necessary expectations for my academics and growth. I was succeeding because they'd made sure I would. This outcome wasn't what they had expected, but the unknown wasn't going to keep them from watching me soar. I kept my excitement to a minimum as best I could.

A few weeks later, I was on an airplane to Washington, D.C., for orientation. I didn't sleep a wink the night before I left. My flight departed at six in the morning, so I made sure the entire family was at Cherry Capital Airport at four a.m. There was *no* way I was going to miss this flight. The program was bringing around one hundred accepted students to D.C. for a week of introductory courses and meetings before we headed off to Germany as newly minted ambassadors. I had been so excited about my adventure to another country, I was unprepared for how meaningful the visit to D.C. was going to be.

Standing in front of the Lincoln Memorial, I stopped to

take a photo with my old, chunky digital camera. I had seen this quintessential American image in my history textbooks and in movies, but now that I was standing on its white marble steps, I felt farther from home than I ever had. D.C. felt like its own country, far removed from the rolling hills and farm fields of Northern Michigan.

The next day, we dressed up to visit the United States Capitol, where I met one of my senators from Michigan, Debbie Stabenow. Senator Stabenow thanked me and the other participants for representing our states and country while abroad. She reminded us how important it was that we put our best foot forward and that we were now ambassadors of our country, which required dedication and discipline. I'm pretty sure I sweated through my dress shirt out of both excitement and fear.

Although some of the students were irritated that we weren't just hopping on a plane right to Europe, I was overwhelmed with how dramatically my life was changing, and I hadn't even left the country yet. It was the first time I had really tasted independence and the freedom to make my own choices, and in a sea of kids mostly like me, I felt at ease to present myself in ways I hadn't felt comfortable doing at home. It was freeing and frightening at the same time. Every night during that first week, I retreated to the lobby of the hotel where we were staying and called my parents to tell them about what I had seen and to let them know how much I missed them. I did my best to hide my nerves, as well as my excitement, since I knew Mom was still struggling with the change.

At the end of orientation week, we loaded onto a tour bus and headed to Washington Dulles International Airport. With each step toward the ticket counter, then the security checkpoint, and, ultimately, the boarding gate, I felt a weight pulling at me, as if everything I was afraid to leave behind were clawing at me, urging me to stay. Nervous and excited, I pushed forward, but as I walked down the jet bridge and approached the airplane, I felt a sickness stir in my stomach. Once I passed through that airplane door, I wouldn't be back on American soil for an entire year. I took a deep breath, looked behind me at the sea of passengers waiting for me to make a move, stepped onto that United Airlines 777 bound for Frankfurt, and didn't look back again.

I stayed awake the entire flight, watching the little airplane icon move slowly across the flight map on the screen in front of me. Four thousand miles makes for a long flight. Luckily, I was seated between two participants I had immediately connected with during orientation. We passed the time by telling one another stories of our hometowns and shared what little information we knew about the villages we were going to live in and the families we were about to meet.

When we landed at the mammoth Frankfurt Airport, I said goodbye to my seatmates and caught a connecting flight to Leipzig. From there, I rode a train for the first time in my life, north to the town of Zerbst. A small group of us would live in and around that little town in north-central Germany for the rest of the summer while we took an intensive and exhausting language course five days a week, before moving to our yearlong host families for the school year.

The train rolled into the station, and we were promptly greeted by a crowd of locals waving German flags and home-made signs that read WILLKOMMEN! We felt like celebrities. I stepped off the train in the hot July sun, wondering if the last twenty-four hours of traveling had made me perhaps a bit too greasy and stinky for a first impression. My host mother was waiting for me on the train platform, and as I rolled my two large suitcases toward the parking lot, I paused to blush while she unlocked her Smart car, an automobile no larger than a golf cart. My suitcases took up the entirety of the car. I think I may have overpacked. Her small car had been baking in the sun while she waited for my arrival. With no air-conditioning available, I rolled my window down to take in the breeze. The scent permeating from my clothes caused me to blush once more. I leaned down to sneak a whiff of my armpit. Oof. Yeah. Definitely needed a shower.

My host family lived in a small village about a three-mile bike ride outside the city, and as soon as I met them, it became clear that my German was not as good as I had thought. We stood awkwardly in the foyer when I arrived, and everyone shook my hand and flashed a nice smile to signal that they weren't going to kill me. Then we stared at one another in silence. I was very conscious of my smell. My mind raced, trying to come up with something, anything, to say. Finally, I spat out some German words I knew were foolproof. "Can I . . . have some . . . juice?" I mumbled in my now-dubious German. They nodded, with perhaps a hint of confusion as to why that would be my very first request and not a shower. Honestly, I was just as confused. But I got the juice, so at least I didn't accidentally ask for something embarrassing or inappropriate. Those mistakes would come later and, naturally, be very public and very humiliating.

My host mother then showed me to my new bedroom. Standing in the mostly empty room, it struck me that I had just thrown out my slightly boring but organized and predictable life for all of this unknown. Here I was, on the other side of the world, far away from my family, far away from my friends, and because I had done this, because I had *wanted this*, I was now responsible for getting to know people whose language I didn't speak very well and whose home I would now be living in. I suppose teaching kids this responsibility was the point of the program, but still. You can study a language for years, but nothing prepares you to thrive in another country like *needing* to speak that language.

My host parents left me alone to unpack my suitcases, and as I started to place my clothes in drawers, I reflected on how my day had begun in a hotel room in Washington, D.C. Now here I was, standing in this little bedroom in a small town in Germany where I would be expected to represent my country, master a new language, stay on top of my grades in a school completely foreign to me, and do it all with a smile.

My new bed was as hard as pronouncing the German word for "ice-skating" (it's *Schlittschuhlaufen*—good luck), but that didn't matter much. I was exhausted. The next morning, I awoke in a fog of jet lag and confusion to see the sun blanketing a room that looked nothing like the one I had been sleeping in for the last seventeen years. I rubbed my eyes, reached for my glasses, and took a few moments to remember where I was. With hair askew and morning breath at peak stink, I made my way down the hallway to the kitchen, still wearing my pajamas. I had so many questions swirling in my head: *Is it okay to be in my pajamas? Is it acceptable to be barefoot in the house? Should I shower before I see everyone? By the way, where is the shower? And, if I find it, how does it work?*

Too late, I arrived in the kitchen to see a fully dressed family sitting around the table in comfortable silence. The dad was reading the newspaper and furled a page down in order to get a good look at me. They were all tall and lanky and shared a certain strawberry-blond, freckled complexion. They didn't say much. They were neat, tidy, and well mannered. (In Germany, you're allowed to drink beer at sixteen years old, so when the program later gathered all the host families and exchange students for a little welcome party, I was excited to try my first. I watched as the other Americans toasted their pints of the local *Bier* with one another. My host family, however, served me orange juice.)

My host mom signaled toward my breakfast, a plate of cold cut meats, cheese, and dark multiseed bread. Nothing like the sugary cereals and bagels I was so used to in America. I felt like a raccoon digging through a dumpster while I ate in front of this neat and tidy group of Germans who were trying their very best not to stare at me as I figured out what to do with these loose pieces of meat and a bread so foreign and healthy-tasting, it was as if scientists had discovered a way to turn vitamins into edible bricks. I used lots of butter. With a mouth full of bread and four Germans staring at me, I forced a smile and said, *"Guten Morgen!"* They all smiled and repeated the morning greeting back to me as if a three-day-old puppy had just let out an adorable little "awooo."

After an ice-cold shower in which I never quite figured out how to make the water warm, my host brother showed me the bicycle I could use to travel into town for my language classes. I huffed my slightly-out-of-shape way down the tree-lined road leading from our little village into the city. Language courses were held in a local school building, a former monastery that dated back five hundred years before the American Declaration of Independence was even signed. It looked like a little castle and felt just as charming (besides the lack of air-conditioning). Just down the street, the hollow shell of a church that had been bombed in World War II towered over the main traffic circle, a reminder of more recent history. On lunch breaks, we would walk to the corner bakery, where the kind woman behind the counter would enthusiastically greet the flock of culture-shocked, carb-loving American teenagers flooding her store each day. We ate *a lot* of pretzels.

In the evenings, I would bike the few kilometers home, have dinner with my family, and then read or study quietly in my room. My host brothers didn't seem to want to hang out with me much—I don't think I was the cool American they'd hoped they'd be getting. I'm sure we would have found some common ground, but my German was weak and they were a little too embarrassed to speak English around me (even though they had been studying English ten years longer than I'd been studying German). "So, uh, what's up?" or "Do you like soccer?" and "Yes, I like soccer"—that was about the extent of my small talk at that point. (Even though I wasn't really that interested in soccer, the Germans were, and this was an easy way to earn a smile.)

Once the language course wrapped up, we left Zerbst to meet our yearlong families. Mine lived in Mecklenburg-Vorpommern, a region in northern Germany bordering the Baltic Sea that was peppered with lakes and farms. I was very excited to move in with them. Before I'd left for Germany, my future host brother had found me on MySpace. (This was 2006, and MySpace was *everyone's* favorite social media platform. You could leave an away message and a song playing on your profile to let everyone know how you were feeling, in a very vague and melodramatic way. Just imagine someone playing an emo or sad song on their profile page with an away message that read: "Wow. Guess you can't trust those who claim to luv you the most." It was SO dramatic! What did they mean? Who stabbed who in the back?)

Things began to get a tad more interesting as soon as I arrived. Since it was still summertime, my host family was very excited to take me to a cabin they owned on a local lake. This sounded good to me; I told them, in my improving but still not great German, that we had lots of lakes where I was from too.

What we *don't* have as much of in Northern Michigan is public nudity.

Anyone who has spent time in Europe may know where this is going, but I didn't at the time; although I'd learned a little about German culture in my five years of studying German back home, I had not been introduced to one particular custom. After a few minutes of small talk and hugs and welcomes, my host father proposed that, since the weather was so perfect, we all take a dip in the lake. We walked down to the dock, and I felt a sense of calm, since the small inland lake was similar to the ones I had grown up with in Traverse City. But just as that calmness arose, my host family—mother, father, and son—stripped completely naked in front of me, then jumped in. I blushed and looked away, apologizing. I had barely been able to change in the company of others in the locker room at school, and here I was, expected to jump into a lake completely unclothed.

"Come on in!" my host mother shouted up to me on the dock.

I was torn: *Am I supposed to do this? No, I cannot do this!* My cheeks flushed as I maintained a nervous smile. The family was swimming away from the dock—I needed to make a decision, and fast! I was not ready for this particular aspect of my German experience, though. (Were there sharks in this lake? Of course not, but aagh!) I shuffled back up to the car, dragged out one of my suitcases, brought it inside the cabin, and dug through everything until I finally found my swimsuit. When I emerged from the house, I saw the family trudging back up the lawn with their towels. Too late.

While toweling off naked right there in front of me (an entire hour after our first meeting), my new host mother said, "Something something eating cake," so I decided to skip a swim to sit down and eat cake with them. In my swimsuit. Them in their towels.

The cake was dry, and so was the conversation.

After they had put their clothes back on, I was still too embarrassed to make eye contact with any of them. I later learned that naked swimming—as well as naked sauna—was part of a larger popular German movement called *Freikörperkultur* (literally, "free body culture"). In a very liberating way, Germans just didn't care about nudity that much.

My host family was very excited to share their home with me and asked many questions about my language course, my home in Traverse City, and my goals for the year. Translating was getting hard as I felt my head start to pound a little. My host brother took over in English and translated my thinking into German for his parents, who didn't speak English as fluently. My shoulders started to relax as much as they could after being exposed to naked swim cake time.

A few times during the year, exchange students from our program would get together for conferences and trips abroad. It was a much-needed respite to see other Americans and catch our breath around teenagers who understood what we were going through. In the evenings, we would all gather in the lobby of our hostel and tell stories and laugh until we couldn't stay awake any longer. There was one guy I felt drawn to more than the others. He was funny and gave me a run for my money as the "life of the party." One night, a group of us were lounging on the couches in the lobby, and while everyone was chatting, he reached over and slapped me on the knee as he laughed at one of my jokes.

RECORD SCRATCH

Based on the onslaught of conflicting emotions that were taking place inside my head after a boy simply touched my knee, it was a miracle I didn't vomit all over the floor right there in front of God and everybody. I was so nervous because not only did I really, really appreciate the attention, but my enjoyment of receiving this attention confirmed what I was so afraid of. *Oh my gosh,* I thought. *Is this what butterflies feel like?*

There was no way of denying that happiness. I *was* gay.

Later that night, as the two of us walked back to our rooms, we leaned in and kissed each other good night. This was not the romantic sort of kissing you see in the movies. Oh, no. This was scary and thrilling and humiliating all at the same time. It wasn't just lips meeting lips; it was more . . . teeth meeting teeth. (Luckily, neither of us had braces.) I think we were both embarrassed about how bad we were at it. Of all the dreams I had dreamt about my first kiss, this couldn't have been further from them.

But then it was over. I'd kissed a boy, and I'd liked it.

I went to bed filled with joy and dread. Part of that dread stemmed from the fact that I sort of had a girlfriend at the time—another American in the program. I hadn't really been in a relationship before, and I think she knew I was gay, even if I wasn't ready to admit it to myself yet. Nothing about our relationship was romantic, but we enjoyed hanging out together and she loved my jokes. We went traveling on the weekends and checked in on each other every day, which made it easy to put a label on things, even though I knew my feelings didn't match that label. I wasn't pretending to like her—she was a wonderful person—but I was obviously pretending to *like* her. I wanted so desperately for this *thing* inside me to be untrue, but it was becoming increasingly clear to me that I wasn't what I was telling myself I had to be, and by lying to myself, I was hurting her, too. I felt terrible about it. I was consumed by my anxieties about being gay, and no matter how loud I screamed or how hard I cried, the truth wasn't going to go away. And that one quick, embarrassing kiss shattered every conceivable doubt I had about who I was.

I was wasting my time in Germany by trying to keep my real self hidden. The point of going abroad was to escape that secretiveness. I was still attached to the idea that if I could just push myself hard enough to date a girl or kiss a girl, I could change. I had run so far away from home to escape my doubts about all that, but what I didn't understand at the time is that you cannot run away from those things. Your truth, your identity, your fears—they all follow you.

The challenges in Germany picked up. As I began to feel more comfortable with myself, I ran into some roadblocks with a series of host families, who all had different reasons for passing me along to the next home. One host brother got into some trouble with substances, the next woman could host me for only a few weeks, and the list goes on. I ended up living with six host families throughout the year. My second-to-last family decided that they didn't want an exchange student anymore, and it really hurt. I was finally adjusting not only to being far away from home, but to all the changes that were imposed on me every few months.

New host family, new school, new friends, new teachers. It was a lot to juggle, and the year slowly started slipping away.

This last rejection came just as I was peeking around the coming-out-of-the-closet door, and I was fearful that if I couldn't find another family to host me, I'd have to go back to the States early. I worried I would never fully come to understand my true self if I was thrust back into the closet without seeing my German adventure through. With just a couple of months left to go, I moved in with my last family, thanks to some tireless advocacy from one of my dearest German friends, Franzi. Franzi was the host sister of one of the other American students in my language course, who took it upon herself to check in with all of us Americans, making sure we experienced everything we could, from good food to good music to perfectly planned, adventurous weekends in new places for which she would play tour guide.

Franzi was a wonderful friend, and very German in every way: she was super straightforward, with a serious sense of humor, and engaged in the typical northern German custom of wearing a raincoat even when it was sunny. She was also focused on being there for people emotionally—a friend who actively listened. No interrupting, no useless advice to fill in the awkward spaces in a hard conversation, no making excuses for things that are inexcusable. She invested in her friendships and made sure the other person knew how valued they were. Franzi convinced this last family to host me, and she made sure I had plans on the weekends and people to hang out with. Even though her English was impeccable, she pushed me to improve my language skills by only speaking German with me until my brain couldn't take it any longer. She was always on my side, and she was a great teacher.

Mutti and Vati (cuter German versions of "Mom" and "Dad"), as I came to call my last set of host parents, made a big effort to make me feel welcomed and loved after a bumpy start to my exchange year. Vati worked in Berlin during the week, so it was often Mutti and me on our own, sitting around the table chatting with her many friends while sharing an elaborate German feast of Wiener schniztel and potatoes or drinking peppermint tea while watching the evening news. Mutti didn't really speak English, so in order to survive under her roof, I had to perfect my German, and fast. She was a lively and loving woman who dyed parts of her hair different shades of red every other week. She was always sending me to school with sweets and making my favorite dishes for dinner even as she demanded I perfect my pronunciation and grammar. It often took me twenty minutes to finish a story at her dinner table because she corrected every word that came out of my mouth.

I missed home desperately, but I was also dreading going back to the States. It felt like something inside me had been torn open in Germany and I couldn't mend it. Franzi sensed this in me, and one day, while we were just sitting around talking about our feelings, like we often did in Mutti's old farmhouse, I told her I felt like something was eating me alive, consuming all my focus, and will. Nervously, I told her that I thought I might be bisexual. She replied, in that lovably direct German way, that being bisexual was okay, and so was just being gay. I didn't have to pretend to be anyone I wasn't, and I could be whoever I *was* around her.

Franzi's honesty was almost profound. "Maybe you're just gay." I'd never heard anyone say it so matter-of-factly before—what do you mean, you can just *be gay*? I had only known it as a terrible fate, something you should resist with all your power. It was striking to hear someone talk about it as if it were just another thing you could *be*, like a redhead or a person who's allergic to beestings. And the best part was, a friend was looking me in the eye and saying that I was loved just as I was, and that nothing about our friendship would change, except now Franzi was offering to help me carry what felt like such a heavy load.

The sun was shining through the old farmhouse windows, and Franzi and I sprang up and hugged each other. I laughed and cried as I hugged her closer.

"It's okay, yeah?" she kept asking.

"It's cool, you're cool, don't worry!" I breathed a huge sigh of relief. "Ugh, let's get some air!"

We jumped on our bikes and rode through town, and the air had never tasted so crisp and clean and pure as it did when I breathed it into lungs that felt like they were letting go of every breath they had held for the last seventeen years. The sunshine warmed our backs and faces as we weaved down tree-lined streets and narrow cobblestoned alleys until we finally came to the park where our friends often gathered for picnics and study sessions full of gossip and ice cream. For once I felt so perfectly free.

With just a few remaining months in Germany, Mutti convinced me to make them count. I quickly learned how to find the cheapest airfare or train tickets for little weekend adventures. I flew to Ireland with some friends for twenty dollars, round trip, on Ryanair. We slept in a questionable hostel room and ate the cheapest pub food we could find. I took a ferry to the United Kingdom just to say I'd been, before hopping right back aboard and returning to Ireland for a night out on the town. One weekend, we took a similarly discounted flight to Paris and ate baguettes and cheese on park benches in between walking what seemed like the entire city. The architecture and museums left me speechless. That night, a pole on my bunk bed in the hostel collapsed, and I rolled onto the floor. All I could do was laugh. It didn't take much to amaze me—I was soaking up as much adventure as I could.

In just one short year, I had gone from an awkward and self-conscious kid driving his geeky minivan to the bowling alley, to an American so assured of his abilities that he could participate in class in a foreign language, jump on a train and head to a new city, order a meal, visit a museum, talk with strangers, and navigate an entirely different world all by himself. I didn't need anyone to tell me how to continue walking through this world and how to bend myself to their expectations.

The year started to wind down, and I knew that once I made it back home, I'd have an important choice to make. Having been away for so long meant I couldn't just go back to how I'd been. My life had changed; my sense of self had changed. I needed that change to follow me home. If I didn't stay true to that, if I didn't bring home that same sense of confidence and love for myself, I knew there was no chance of me making it.

I took a deep breath as I stepped off the small regional jet at Cherry Capital Airport. I drew in the thick summer humidity pouring in from the gap between the airplane door and the jet bridge. As I made my way down the arrivals ramp, I saw my entire family and a small group of friends anxiously waiting for me with signs, flowers, and balloons. There they all were, the people I loved the most. A group of people who had seen a different Chasten off to Germany, and now, I feared, might turn their backs on the one coming home. Mom came running toward me with her arms stretched as wide as she could. "My baby!" she shouted as she drew me in for the biggest hug she could muster. She leaned her forehead onto mine and stared into my eyes, taking in the tearful young man who had returned to her. She covered my cheeks in kisses. She just couldn't let me go. I loved seeing her this happy. I loved this feeling. I was overwhelmed with how good it felt to be so wanted and welcomed and loved by my family and friends. I hugged each and every one of them. So much had changed. There was so much they didn't know. We made our way to the baggage claim. I stood anxiously among all of them, happy to be back in their orbit, and nervous about what came next. Was I really about to throw this all away?

8

Running

When I was in Germany, I stood out for obvious reasons: I was American and I spoke German imperfectly. Compared to the ways I stood out or didn't blend in at home, being a foreigner with an accent wasn't a big deal. My Americanness was awkward, but not a real problem. In fact, I was in Germany to "promote cultural exchange" between Germany and the States, so my difference was actually a *good* thing. On top of that, when friends or peers in Germany noticed the things that made me stand out back home, they didn't seem to care. There were far more students who were comfortable being "out" in Germany than there were back in Michigan. In Germany, I learned that being gay didn't necessarily mean the same things to everyone as it did to the people in my conservative community at home. Sure, there were some awkward moments and interactions when this was discussed, especially among the older generations, but for the most part, people in Germany moved on with their lives when they learned someone was gay—they didn't see someone else's orientation as any of their business in the first place.

I had attempted to date a girl and failed. I had come out to a friend and succeeded. The former made me feel guilty and horrible, and the latter gave me hope that maybe there could be love in my future, something I had assumed from a young age was never going to happen. This realization about the relative insignificance of being gay, plus the distance that had allowed me the opportunity to come to terms with who I am, allowed me to return home understanding that, yes, this is me and that I needed to get better at loving myself and accepting myself for who I truly am. I was ready to focus on other parts of my life rather than let this one tiny detail about who I am have such a strong control over my happiness and my future.

Coming to terms with being gay was really hard. It wasn't like a switch was flipped and I immediately thought, *All right! This is who I am! Bring it on, world!* In fact, I was a complete mess. Whatever joy and confidence I'd gained from being accepted into the exchange program, making friends in a foreign country, and coming out to myself were contaminated by my belief that my family and community were not going to accept the new me once I came home. As

soon as I had gotten a little comfortable admitting what I'd
realized about myself, I had to go back to a life where a lot
of people made me feel I had to keep it a secret. It seemed
that I could either be honest and risk losing everything or
continue living with this fundamental part of myself hidden. Basically, the worst kind of secret agent. The stress of
making either choice gnawed at me day in and day out. I was
proud of what I was feeling inside—that I was slowly learning to love and accept myself. But if I embraced this self that
I was learning to love, how much would I lose because of it?
And if I did lose everything, would I still feel that pride and
love for myself, knowing that I'd broken my parents' hearts
and disappointed my friends and family?

Leaving during my senior year of high school had
already been hard on my parents, and now I was preparing to
disappoint them once more. Coming out of the closet would
not only sadden them; it would also confirm their suspicions
that venturing outside Traverse City wasn't a good idea. *He
shouldn't have gone,* they'd think. *The Europeans must have
corrupted him!* If they took me seriously, would they think
I was a sinner or a failure who deserved to be cast out? If
they decided my coming out was just a phase, they would
be denying all the pain I'd already felt about myself and the
very real trauma of growing up being told that homosexu-
ality was a mistake and an abomination in the eyes of God.
The prospect of being doubted or waved away was humiliating. I felt totally trapped.

This is a trap many LGBTQ+ Americans find themselves in, particularly those living in rural, conservative places where it might not be as safe to be "different." Most often, the fear of rejection, or even violence, pushes people further into the closet and forces them to hide their truest self from those who don't believe that LGBTQ+ people are equal citizens, worthy of being treated equally and with dignity. This is often made worse by those in positions of power who don't seek to learn or understand and instead weaponize and demonize LGBTQ+ people against other Americans. Our community is unfortunately still used as a scapegoat by those who demean and attack vulnerable people in order to benefit from attention and conflict, rather than work on important issues that actually affect people's lives. In many places, it is simply unsafe for people to be out, and that is exacerbated in places where politics have made life harder than it already is through backward and hateful legislation.

We know that students who go to a school or live in a home that is accepting and affirming are *far* less likely to suffer from mental health crises and conflict. This is why it is essential to make sure that LGBTQ+ people know they are welcomed and accepted in our families, friend groups, schools, and beyond. We all must do our best to work toward a world in which all people, especially youths, can thrive and, therefore, *survive*.

While traveling the country on behalf of my husband's

presidential campaign, I met couples who had been together longer than I've been alive, tearful to see me in person as the spouse of an openly gay man running for president. I didn't have to say much of anything—the simple fact that Peter and I existed was, to some, a miracle. But then they'd lean in and tell me they're not out. *They couldn't be.* Sometimes they would tell me that they had driven for hours to attend one of my visits, out of excitement, yes, but also just for the safety of distance. They couldn't risk anyone seeing them attending an event for the gay candidate or even holding one of our pride-themed PETE placards, out of fear of retribution. These interactions always left me with such a strong sense of obligation and gratitude. Even if it seems like things are getting much better for some, I was reminded of just how painful homophobia and exclusion can be, especially in areas of our country where inclusion hasn't arrived as fast as in other places.

I came home from Germany in the summer of 2007, graduated from high school, and prepared to start classes at the local community college in the fall. I'd settled on attending Northwestern Michigan College in Traverse City. Mom was pleased that I was staying closer to home. It was a step forward and, ultimately, a wise one. I wanted to feel secure in who I was and know that it was all going to be okay before I went off to university. To be honest, for a while, I wasn't even sure I was going to make it to college.

With all the progress I had made in Germany sitting in the back of my head, shouting at me to embrace my identity and lean into being truthful about who I was, I still, somehow, painfully, told myself to try, just one more time, to make being straight work. Cue: Ella.

Ella and I had been hanging out all summer, and I knew right away that I was making a big mistake by allowing her to believe that our relationship was romantic. She was sweet, funny, and curious. We'd go for long walks, talk for hours on the phone, and debate the big questions with each other over coffee and dinner. One evening, as we sat on the beach, we cuddled close on our blanket as a late-summer sun dipped below the horizon on Grand Traverse Bay. With the summer tourists long gone, the beach was ours, and we took in the postcard view as waves rolled slowly onto the sand and the seagulls filled the air with their annoying yet charming screeches. The temperature was dropping, so we cuddled even closer. If this had been a movie featuring me as the handsome prince waiting for the perfect time to kiss the girl, THIS WAS THE MOMENT, CHASTEN!

The evening was perfect. Ella looked at me and smiled. I smiled in return. But then I looked back at the water.

Ella leaned into me as if to nudge me along, signaling that I should probably lean over and kiss her—make this relationship an official love story. I turned my head back toward her. She smiled another delicate smile as the sunset glowed in her hair. She was beautiful and deserving of everything she wanted from me. I returned the smile again and . . . turned back toward the water once more.

The movie score could build for only so long—humming, swelling, waiting to give way to the crashing of a string-filled melody as the young lovers finally share a romantic kiss under the color-streaked summer sunset. But I couldn't do it.

"Aren't you going to kiss me?" she asked. Her question was hopeful, but her face told me she already knew the answer. A very long conversation followed.

Rather than expressing disappointment or selfishness, Ella made space for me to (clumsily) come out to her on my own terms. Once she saw all the pain pouring out of my body in tears, she pulled me in closer. Our friendship, thank goodness, remained. Like Franzi, Ella provided me with a safe space to be myself, and after our talk on the beach, I slowly started coming out to more of my close friends. Sometimes by blurting it out; sometimes by saying it nonchalantly, as if I were talking about the weather. I didn't have a recipe to follow, so I just winged it.

Those earlier conversations with supportive friends made it easier to slowly come out to those I felt I could trust. Opening up about my truth hardly ever went perfectly, though. Even if some people understood, I could sense nervousness in their support of me—it was still unsafe, and difficult, to be gay in Traverse City. Coming out started to feel like a press tour for a new movie. I'd have sit-downs, phone calls, and group chats with friends in order to get this big weight off my chest. I felt nauseated when I told my close friends; still, I knew that being gay was okay—not some kind of incurable disease. Now the scary part was whether my friendships would last.

Sometimes my conversations weren't as receptive as I'd hoped for.

"This is not what God wants for you, Chasten."

Tori's words came rippling through the phone like fire into my ear. How could someone who'd known me since middle school all of a sudden decide I wasn't worthy of friendship anymore? Tori continued, "I'm just really disappointed in you. It's a sin. Like, I love you and stuff, but it's a sin. I'm sorry."

I love you and stuff. I kept playing those words over and over in my head. I didn't understand. How could someone say they loved me and then tell me I was going to hell just for being the way God had made me? It was like suggesting that someone was going to hell for sneezing. You don't choose that! It just happens!

It is quite silly that LGBTQ+ people need to publicly come out, isn't it? Imagine if straight people had to come out—we'd be overwhelmed with constant announcements and parties! It took me a while to learn this lesson, but when it comes to coming out, you don't owe anybody anything. Your story is your story, and yours alone. You are not required to tell anyone, because it's none of their business. Coming out can be really freeing for some people, like it was for me, and for others, it can be terrifying and invasive. You get to decide if, how, and when you want to come out to other people.

With a few friends supporting me, I inched closer to working up the courage to tell Mom and Dad. It's a small town, and word travels fast around these parts. I didn't want anyone beating me to it. (By the way, just like it's your decision to share your coming-out story, someone else's story is *most definitely not yours to tell*.) I didn't concoct an elaborate plan about how to break the news to Mom and Dad—this wasn't a time for celebration, and there was no way to make it perfect. I anticipated that my life would implode as soon as it was over. Mom and Dad had raised me for eighteen years, and those years had been full of hopes and dreams for how I might turn out and who I would become. I was about to blow all of that up. I loved my parents very much, but I had a firm belief that I would be loved only conditionally in return once I revealed this truth. *Nobody hopes for a gay child,* I thought.

This turned out to be completely unfair of me, but at the time, I thought for sure that my coming out would be an immense disappointment to my parents. I felt like I was destroying the dream they'd had for me: that I'd get a good job, marry a woman, and live nearby so that they would have full access to spoiling their grandkids. In those days, being gay didn't just mean I wouldn't marry a woman—it meant not getting married at all. Marriage equality was not decided upon by the US Supreme Court until 2015, eight years after I came out. Therefore, having kids or a family as a gay man seemed all but impossible.

I had decided I would have to leave home after I came out to my parents, and I knew that, once I left, there was no telling if I'd come back. I'd given a friend the heads-up that I planned on telling my parents, and she told me that if I needed a place to go afterward, I could come sleep at her house. I told her she should definitely expect me, because I wasn't sure my parents were going to handle it well. I stayed up the entire night before, wondering how there could be anything next for me, counting down the hours until I lost everything I knew.

I drove home and found the house mostly empty. Mom was in the kitchen when I came up the stairs. I didn't stop as I murmured, "Hi, Mom."

"Hi, Bubby."

I always knew she was in a good mood when she used my nickname.

Am I really about to do this to her?

I went straight to my bedroom and closed the door behind me. I knelt on the floor of my childhood bedroom as I haphazardly stuffed clothes into a bag I had pulled from underneath my bed. The same black-and-red backpack that I had traveled across Europe with just months earlier. The photos and awards hanging on the wall—4-H blue ribbons, theater opening nights, bowling plaques—reminded me of the child Mom and Dad had known for so long. Now, I thought, I was going to upend everything they thought I was. Once I did, would I be a stranger to them?

I never considered the freedom I'd feel once I was able to be myself in front of my parents and family. I never fantasized about meeting a guy, falling in love, and living a long, happy life together. Eighteen-year-old Chasten didn't think there was any chance this heavy weight would be lifted. Instead, I feared everything was about to get a lot heavier.

Our dogs scratched at my bedroom door. I cracked it open, and they came rushing in, sniffing around my bag, sensing something was up. I collected myself as best I could and walked into our living room holding the letter I had written for my parents. I don't remember exactly what it said, but I clearly remember the scene. Mom was now sitting in the recliner, watching TV, folding bath towels. The windows were open. It was sunny outside, and the wind was blowing through the screened windows. The dogs circled in the room as I tearfully, shakily, handed her the letter. Dad wasn't there, but I couldn't muster the courage to wait for him. She looked at me with a smile, as if I were handing her a gift, but as she slowly read it, the look on her face changed. When she was done, she looked up and began to cry.

She asked if I was sure about "this." Yes, I answered, I *was* sure. She asked if I was sick; I think she thought that maybe I had AIDS (acquired immunodeficiency syndrome), a deadly illness stemming from HIV (human immunodeficiency virus), which prevents the body from fighting infections. HIV/AIDS ravaged the gay community in the late '80s, killing generations of gay and bisexual people. Because HIV/AIDS was affecting primarily gay people, the government was very slow to get involved, since it was unsupportive of the LGBTQ+ community in general. HIV/AIDS is still prevalent today, but there are new and evolving medicines that are allowing patients to live longer, healthier lives. Despite this, HIV in the LGBTQ+ community and beyond still faces much stigmatization.

I told Mom no, I wasn't sick—nothing was wrong.

I ran out of things to say except that I was sorry, so I picked up my bag and I left.

Now, what comes next is not my parents' fault. I don't believe it was my fault, either, but the crucial thing to remember is that, while they have come a long way from what they believed when I first I came out, my parents never kicked me out. They never said, Get out—you're not my son. In fact, my mother was mad that I was so set on leaving. Moments after I walked out the door, she called my cell and demanded to know why.

"Where are you going?" she pleaded. "Why did you leave?"

I remember driving away from my parents' home, crying so forcefully that I worried the tears would prevent me from seeing the road. It was the kind of crying that you feel so deep in your chest that your lungs burn as you gasp for air. Every word needed a separate breath. "I'm . . . so . . . sorry . . . Mom," I said. "I'm . . . so . . . sorry . . . to . . . do . . . this . . . to . . . you."

I'm sure my parents were confused and frustrated by my explanation at the time, but I felt that I was such a disappointment that I couldn't stand to be in the house.

This is how homophobia works, and a product of homophobia is internalized homophobia—meaning that even gay people can begin to hate themselves after they've been told they're undeserving of love and acceptance because of who they are. I left home because I was so embarrassed of myself that I had to get away from my family; I assumed that they were mad at me, that they wouldn't want to talk about it unless I somehow took it back. I couldn't stop thinking about all their conservative friends from church: though my parents weren't the type to talk about their religion or try to convert others to it, they had friends who were and who did, and once those friends found out, I thought my parents would feel burdened by all the uncomfortable, scolding conversations they were going to have to have about me. I knew it would be an embarrassment that would haunt my family, and I didn't want to inflict that on anyone.

That first night away from home, I slept on my friend's couch, and after a couple of days, she set up an inflatable mattress in her office for me. She was studying for her master's degree at the time, and I'd have to deflate my mattress and move my things out of the way each morning so she could get to her desk to work. I was working full-time and, later that fall, attending my first college classes. Sometimes, when I felt I was too much of a burden on her, I'd just sleep in my car to stay out of the way. The back seat of my Saturn Ion was no five-star hotel, but there was solitude and some much-needed space away from all the noise and guilt. Sleeping in the back of my car was lonely, but being alone was what I needed at the time. Even though it felt like a safe option, it wasn't, and it was a very risky choice. Many of my friends today, when they hear this part of my story, are upset that I didn't reach out to them and that they didn't know the pain I was going through.

If I wasn't in class or at work, I'd often drive my car aimlessly around town just to feel like I was headed somewhere. This inner battle of guilt, shame, and sleepless nights went on for a couple of months, until one day my mom called and asked me to come home. "Just come home and we'll figure it out, Bubby," she said. I drove straight to my parents' house. Mom met me at the top of the stairs and hugged me as close as she could. I hadn't exhaled in months.

Early on in my coming-out journey, I remember my mother saying, "I just don't know why you would choose something so hard." Even though I know my mother meant well, her response reflects the attitude that well-meaning but less-informed people most often have when their kids come out: Why would I *choose* to be made fun of and demeaned and picked on? Why would I give up the possibility of family, "real" love, and a career? Why would I choose something that got people killed? I knew she wanted to protect me as best she could.

But here's where my good fortune truly saved me. Even though it took a little bit of time, my coming-out story has a happy ending, and that has made a world of difference. My parents welcomed me back into their home. My mom and dad asked questions and listened to me, and they invited me to give feedback, even when it was hard for them to receive. Once they really understood, my parents could see that being gay was just who I was, that it wasn't a choice for me, that it was something I was born with, and something completely out of their control. They hadn't done anything wrong. What *was* a choice was that we all decided to discuss it in good faith, to not jump to conclusions or accusations or fall back on stereotypes that had no basis in fact or experience.

A few months after I came out to my parents, I decided it was time to tell the only living grandparent I had. Wanda, my mother's mother, was a force to be reckoned with. She was a deeply religious woman, a devout Catholic who took tradition and family very seriously (though she'd sometimes lean over while we were kneeling and praying in church to tell me to keep walking after we took Communion so we could beat the other families to the restaurant for breakfast. She loved her god, but she also loved not waiting for a table at Cracker Barrel). I adored my grandmother. I spent a lot of time with her growing up, and in high school, I'd often stop by to check in on her for a few minutes, which usually turned into Mom calling to tell me to come home for dinner. I'd sit on Grandma's couch and listen to her tell stories about growing up in Oklahoma and how her father would make her pick cotton out in the fields. She'd tell me about the cherry farm or my mom's childhood. Grandma always lured me in with a root beer or something sweet, and we'd sit and watch television or talk. I know we're not supposed to play favorites, but I think I was pretty high up on her list.

One evening, while Grandma was visiting, I asked if I could take a walk with her. We made our way outside and eventually found ourselves sitting in the front seat of her Buick Skylark. We sat in silence, and I stared at her rosary dangling from the rearview mirror. The tears began to well as I thought about breaking her heart. I looked over at her confused expression—she could tell I was hurting. "Grandma, I . . ." But I choked. She immediately reached her hand over and rested it on my forearm. I felt her rings pressing deep into my arm as I struggled to get any words out. "I know, Chassers," she said. "And I love you just the same." I laughed and fell apart in her arms, catching my breath while inhaling her perfume from the sleeve of her sweater. How long had she known and waited for me to tell her? She brushed a few fingers through my hair and hushed my tears, telling me it was going to be all right.

Grandma was my staunchest ally. She died less than two months after I married Peter. Our wedding was the last trip she took outside of Traverse City. Her lungs were working overtime at the wedding as she walked slowly down the aisle of the church, her mobile oxygen tank puffing and echoing through the small sanctuary as she struggled to breathe. From the lectern, Grandma looked into our eyes as she read the Gospel (Matthew 5:13–16), which instructed us to go out and let our light shine for all the world to see. She beamed with pride at me as I gripped Peter's hand tightly. I was so lucky to be loved by her.

Being gay did not prevent me from having that beautiful moment on my wedding day. Being gay didn't prevent me from finding love, happiness, or family. But like many who have walked a similar path, it did take a while for me to discover that those things were possible—much longer than it needed to.

Looking back on my journey, I know I was lucky in so many ways. It isn't uncommon to hear of people in the LGBTQ+ community losing their friends, their families, and their livelihoods when they come out. Historically, you could not work for the American federal government if you were gay, or perceived to be gay, because it was assumed that gay people were not to be trusted. Yes, they actually thought gay people were spies.

Obviously, things have changed. But the sheer amount of time and energy I devoted to coming out and coming to terms with my true self prevented me from focusing on other crucial aspects of my young adult life. Of course, I don't regret coming out at all; I couldn't stand being in the closet, so I don't feel as if things could have gone any differently. But for those first few years after I did, I couldn't see much more than a couple of steps in front of me.

One of my biggest regrets about those years is that I was so hard on myself. Even after Mom called me home and some of my closest friends committed to being there for me, I couldn't easily switch my brain off from those nervous and scared feelings that told me to run. That's called "flight, fight, or freeze." When faced with danger or trauma, people typically have an instinct to do one of those actions. I was living in a vicious cycle of all three. (Internalized homophobia strikes again!) I never stopped to consider what *I* believed, what *I* thought, or what *I* wanted. It was so hard to quiet that awful voice in the back of my head that reminded me of all the ways in which the world and this small town just weren't ready for someone like me. *Surely I don't have value,* I thought. *My feelings and emotions are not valid, so I shouldn't burden other people with them.*

Those first few months after running from home were blurry. A few weeks after I'd returned from Germany, I picked up a job at Cherry Republic, which, you may remember, is the region's source (and tourist trap) for all things cherry. Later that fall, I settled on what I was going to study in school. I had dreamt of a career in the theater arts, but I allowed myself to believe it was out of reach, so I decided to study nursing and go into healthcare. I had watched Mom pour so much love and passion into her nursing assistant career at the hospital, and I was excited to learn how to care for people myself. As college rolled on and I became more confident in my abilities, I got a job as a home health aide working with a nonverbal sixteen-year-old boy with cerebral palsy.

I really enjoyed working with him. Giving back and helping others feel good about themselves became a great way for me to feel good about *myself*. I'd meet him at his bus stop and take him home, and his daily stretching session coincided perfectly with when *Ellen* came on TV. We'd laugh together at all her jokes. On the weekends, we'd go on adventures to the bowling alley or the movie theater. It was a great job that proved to me that I had what it took to take care of other people. Soon, a job as a nursing assistant at the hospital became available. It was a hard job to land— the pay was competitive, especially when I was able to pick up overtime on overnight shifts—so I transitioned out of my Cherry Republic and home health aide jobs so I could take it.

My responsibilities at the hospital required taking patients' vital signs (like their blood pressure, temperature, and heart rate), helping them to and from the bathroom, and a lot of cleaning—both rooms and people. On my floor, many patients had had surgery, and I liked being the nice guy who came in and made them laugh while they were down or hurting. Many nurses liked me because I was careful and detail-oriented, but I wasn't annoying about it. Or maybe I was. All I know is, they never yelled at me for occasionally eating the ice cream that was supposed to be for patients. I could sense I was onto something at the hospital.

Sustaining a full-time job at the hospital was the easy part; navigating college while trying to figure out where I was headed on my own personal path was another thing. Neither of my brothers had lasted very long in college, and as first-generation college students, we didn't know as much going in as some of our peers whose parents had also gone to college. Despite everything my parents had done to try to prepare me for a life after school, college wasn't necessarily the easiest puzzle to solve. The college experience certainly goes much smoother if you're equipped with mentors, an understanding of money, and a game plan.

I was starting to fall behind in the "school" part of nursing school. If I'd been at a different point in my life, I probably would have finished, but I wasn't talking to my family at first, and then, even after I went home, I was still in survival mode. I was trying to figure out who I was, and I couldn't focus because I was so exhausted from working full-time and, for a while, not having a stable place to sleep. I was also slowly starting to dip my toe into the dating scene, which, as anyone who's done it knows, is no simple feat. Though

I had started to find a community of other gay people in Traverse City, I also seemed to attract people who wanted to take advantage of me. This added a layer of exhaustion to my already-exhausted state.

I decided I needed a change.

With some community college credits under my belt and with the stability of having my parents back in my life helping me feel slightly more secure, I transferred to the University of Wisconsin–Milwaukee. I found a house that I could share with three or four other guys; it had an illegal bedroom in the attic—you just had to walk through an unfinished part (carefully) to get to it. There was no heating or cooling system, so I would have to use a space heater and descend a rickety staircase to use the bathroom. No big deal. I had wilderness skills. I wanted something completely different from what I knew, and I was going to get it.

Wilderness skills did not prepare me for having to cover utility bills and for roommates who didn't pay their share or wash their dishes. By the time I got to classes for nursing, I was seriously behind. After just one semester at UWM, I failed, miserably, and came back home, once again ashamed that I couldn't prove that the life I wanted could work out. I moved back in with my parents, reenrolled in the community college, and got a job at Toys "R" Us, where my job mostly involved asking customers pointless questions as their screaming kids demanded to play with the toys they were about to pay for. *Would you like to sign up for a two-year warranty for your cheap light-up toy? Would you like to join our birthday program? Can I interest you in some batteries for that obnoxiously loud electronic action figure that's going to ruin your life?* Because the customers disliked this as much as I did, they usually responded by yelling at me and saying things to a nineteen-year-old college kid that I probably shouldn't write in a book. I had to work on Black Friday, the busiest shopping day of the year. Enough said.

At some point, I decided that part of my inability to focus was because I wasn't following my true passions. I thought of all the teachers who'd encouraged me to be practical, and then I decided, no. *I'm going to study theater, because that's where I've always felt like I belong.* I looked at going back to Wisconsin and found a way to get a discount on tuition at the University of Wisconsin–Eau Claire, where I enrolled as a theater major. I hadn't been that excited in a very long time. I was putting myself first, and I didn't care who said it was impractical. I needed to chase a dream for once.

By now, I had lots and lots of random credits and an impressive amount of student debt. My decision to go to college at Eau Claire wasn't very well thought out, and I made it based on assumptions that didn't really match reality. I didn't want to be at home. I was embarrassed to go to a school with my childhood friends; I think I was afraid of rejection or being judged for not doing college the "right way." I wanted to be far away. And looking at my options realistically, the best getaway for me wasn't under the shining lights of New York's Times Square, but in a small town in northern Wisconsin.

Determined as ever, I packed up everything I could fit into the back of my Saturn and drove north, ready to try, to make my dream of graduating from college come true.

9

How to Succeed in Wisconsin without Really Crying

Driving a car with an exterior that is primarily constructed from plastic is not the wisest decision in the harsh, Midwestern winters. Making my way north on I-94 from Madison to Eau Claire to check out the campus before making my enrollment official, snow whipped across the windshield as I felt the tires grab what they could of the ice-covered roads. *What the heck am I doing?* I thought. Fifteen hours after I had set out from Traverse City (that gorgeous Lake Michigan really gets in the way if you're needing to head west), my little Saturn rolled into the small college town ninety miles east of Minneapolis. I didn't know it at the time, but Eau Claire, Wisconsin, has a lot more to offer than freezing cold weather and good cheese; it was about to change my life forever.

As soon as I arrived, I felt like I'd found a little shelter from the storm. While touring the theater department with Dr. Chapman, my soon-to-be college advisor and mentor, we entered the greenroom (*much* nicer than the one from my Wonka concussion), where a group of students was holding a meeting for the student-run theater group (of which I would one day become vice president), the UWEC Players. Dr. Chapman introduced me to the cohort of misfits who were about to become some of my closest friends. I was immediately invited for coffee (Midwestern hospitality at its finest). We layered up with hats and coats and headed down the snow-blanketed riverwalk that lined the campus until we arrived at a small coffee shop, Racy D'Lenes, where my new friends asked me endless questions about home, Germany, and what I wanted out of UWEC. *Where have these people been all my life?* I wondered.

The loudest, funniest, and most inviting of all the crew was Eddie. He was studying nursing and theater, was recently out of the closet (but far braver and self-assured than I was at the time), and was directing the upcoming production of a student-written play. "Auditions are tonight. You coming or what, Michigan?" he snapped. It didn't take much convincing for me to stick around another day so I could audition. Later that night, the herd of us piled into booths at a local pub. Eddie told me he would offer me a role, a straight businessman (can you imagine?), opposite a quiet but warm girl named Olivia. The rest, as they say, is history.

I'd always felt like theater was a safe space, and finding it at this moment in my life was a much-needed relief. Although I still didn't feel at all sure that this track would lead to a successful career after college, I was craving community and the opportunity to grow, and Eau Claire was willing to provide what I needed in order to flourish. Theater was where I felt most at home, and I was going to do my best to feel at home again.

I returned to Traverse City, packed up my things, and was back in Eau Claire as soon as a dorm room became available. I arrived on campus during the winter break before most students returned for spring classes. Holding the keys to my very own dorm room, I was filled with pride and energized to give this college thing my all one last time. I put the key in the lock, turned the handle, and smiled as I opened the door to my next chapter.

My smile quickly evaporated as I was met with a smell so foul, I couldn't decipher if it was the spoiled milk on the desk or the dirty socks stewing in the bag of dirty gym gear over in the corner. Rotting food sat in the garbage can, and mildew-covered towels hung from the empty bunk that was supposed to be mine. Without setting my bags down, I marched back to the housing office and asked for a different placement. I figured they would say something like, *Suck it up, kid, this is college!* But, hey, you've got to advocate for yourself, right? Luck was on my side. An empty room was available, complete with a view of the icy river that divided campus and the footbridge that led to the Haas Fine Arts Center—my new home for the semester. I unpacked my things and then made my way back to the coffee shop, where the small group of theater students were waiting to welcome me.

As I settled in, I felt like I was finally on a path headed somewhere. One evening, Dr. Chapman invited me into her office to chat after a rehearsal. I hadn't come out to any of my classmates just yet, but Dr. Chapman could sense I needed some guidance and, perhaps, a friend to talk to. After weeks of late-night postrehearsal office chats with her, I said, "I think you know something about me." She smiled. It was the first time someone outside my small group of friends back home was giving me the space to open up about what I was feeling. There was a lot I needed to unburden myself of, and she let me dump it all onto her desk. Dr. Chapman's mentorship and friendship pushed me through the rest of college and, eventually, grad school and beyond.

For a few weeks that first semester, I would pass the greenroom at the theater but not go in, unsure I'd be welcomed into what seemed like the most exclusive of clubs. But I was so sorely mistaken—I just had to make the effort to get out there and make friends. When I sat in the greenroom, I would look around and marvel at the cast of characters I had stumbled upon. I was finally making friends who were genuine and easy to talk to and who loved me for me—yes, the goofy parts, but also the rough parts in need of smoothing.

We enjoyed a good laugh, but we could also stay up all night debating deep philosophical questions about love and life, or comparing notes on childhood trauma or new crushes. Kathy was inimitable: we would often finish each other's sentences and communicate across the room using birdcalls or accents so ridiculous, you'd wonder if we'd caught some sort of hallucination-inducing fever. How freeing it was to be so loud and goofy and *me*! Riley was crafty and quick with the pen, and he'd often host theater students at his apartment for board games and lounge sessions in which we'd spill our guts crying or laugh until we peed our pants. One night we tried to use a Ouija board, but we lost interest and ordered Domino's pizza instead.

Siri was full of energy and well-timed humor; her laugh could be heard from down the hallway as she launched into a dramatic monologue, usually accusing someone of a crime they hadn't committed, just to get a rise out of them. Marissa could pile on to the running joke being tossed around the greenroom like a ball the moment she entered the room, as if this were all one big scripted sitcom. And Grace was always prepared for anything—studying late at night in the library or being irresponsible and going to the Mexican restaurant across the street for giant burritos the fifth time that week. It was difficult to be in public with any of them—we were much too loud and unbearable to adhere to any public norms. In fact, the only time I've ever been kicked out of a restaurant was with this band of characters. (We weren't disturbing the peace *thaaaaat* much, I swear.) Whether we were sharing a meal, working on an intense project at two in the morning, or taking a bow on the closing night of a play, these people were so dear and caring and close to my heart, I never wanted that feeling of home to disappear.

Once I worked up the courage to come out to them, nobody blinked an eye. I had spent my first two years of college believing that I didn't belong, but more than that, I had also convinced myself I was unworthy of the big things I was chasing in Eau Claire. Now I was surrounded by a support system so strong, I couldn't imagine my time with them ending.

While my life wasn't feeling empty anymore, my bank account sure was! College is expensive and requires much more than tuition and books. College today costs about 150 percent more than it did when my parents' generation attended. Whereas they could go to school and afford tuition, books, and housing on a part-time salary, students nowadays can spend just on books the same amount their parents spent on an entire degree. Needless to say, college is unaffordable these days. I started taking out loans when I enrolled in the community college in Traverse City after high school, and I had *no* idea what I was getting myself into. I took the words "financial aid" at face value: I needed aid with my finances, so I went to an office and requested just that. I couldn't understand how other people made it all work. The arithmetic was very simple: the money I earned working part-time at the hospital was less than the total cost of all my tuition bills, and expenses. But there were *always* more unexpected costs. Like when the Mitsushitzu met its fiery end that first semester back home, forcing me to find a new way to get to and from classes and work. We're talking about Northern Michigan and Wisconsin here for my college career, both of which had unreliable (and often nonexistent) public transportation options; not having a car made life very difficult for someone working and going to school full-time.

The nice folks working at the financial aid office told me I could take out a student loan to pay for books, gas, tuition, and whatever else I needed, so I borrowed a couple thousand dollars. Owing that amount of money was manageable, and since I'd always worked as much as I could in high school, I had no reason to assume I'd run into any problems throughout my college years. I just needed a little help starting out.

Unfortunately, like so many others in my generation, I found out that just getting on my feet cost a lot more than I'd imagined. After my first semester in the dorms in Eau Claire, I moved into town, and even though renting an apartment was cheaper than room and board at school, it would cost me first and last month's rent, along with a security deposit for potential damages (that was three months' worth of rent!) up front. Then there was the visit to the college bookstore, where five hundred dollars for textbooks and supplies was considered a good deal. By the time I'd make it to the grocery store, my wallet would be begging me to stop.

Mom taught me a lot about using coupons and stretching a dollar at the grocery store. Nothing screamed saving money more than the infamous peanut butter and jelly sandwich. Mom was known for cutting costs, but growing up, Jif peanut butter was an absolute must for Dad. When Mom met Dad in high school, he was living off peanut butter sandwiches. Dad worked at a diner and lived in a trailer with a friend south of town, and he would often walk to and from school and then work each day if and when his untrusty motorcycle broke down. He didn't have much money when he met my mom. She would later tell me about how Dad would keep his coat on at school every day because he couldn't always afford to take his clothes to a laundromat to wash them. The year they met, Mom made him the first birthday cake he had ever had, with candles and his name on it. Another way Mom and Dad taught us you didn't need much money to get by or to make a home.

Dad always insisted that Jif was the best peanut butter, so if you had Jif peanut butter on the shelf, you were doing just fine. Eventually, after years of hearing him repeat this, I learned to appreciate this lesson in modesty and saving money. In fact, I have two tattoos: one for Mom, an infinity symbol on my right calf, which I got after she found out she had a rare form of skin cancer, and one for Dad, the colors of the Jif label on my left arm. (Most people think this is a joke, but it's real!)

Figuring out how to make it all work on my own became

a job in and of itself. *Why wasn't this taught in high school?* I thought. I would sit in class nervously wondering if the tips I made from the random, part-time jobs I picked up were going to cover my bills. That's a lot of stress when you're supposed to be "focusing on studying." I thought that going to college was what I was supposed to do and that taking out loans was how I was supposed to pay for what government aid didn't cover.

I wanted to prove that I could do it all by myself. I just expected that once I graduated, I'd have a job and pay it all back, because that's what everyone else seemed to believe. The student loan providers' cheerful assurances that they had my back did nothing to suggest otherwise. But that's not how it works.

I see now that my experience with money was so naïve. When I was growing up, I trusted that saving and spending was a process that would work out if I was careful and hard-working, because that was what my parents had taught me. The fact is that most people can't afford to spend an extra few thousand dollars (at best) every few months for several years, and most people can't afford to decrease their hours at work to give themselves more time to study.

Younger generations are continuously blamed for falling victim to this false promise. "If only they'd stop buying five-dollar lattes" is a common argument for the reason why some young people can't get ahead in life. I know firsthand that making ends meet is more complicated than spending less on, say, coffee. It's also quite silly to suggest that a burger or Frappuccino is what's holding young people back from financial stability when they're paying hundreds of thousands of dollars more for education and housing. Besides, sometimes it's nice to just indulge in a pumpkin spice latte when life's bigger pleasures (owning a home, higher education, finding love, a sense of possibility) feel like they'll remain out of reach forever.

Despite all of the real-world issues keeping me up at night, I was still thriving in the theater community at UWEC, and I was so happy to have found the college experience I'd seen on TV and in movies, with all the curiosity, great memories, and lifelong friends I'd imagined. I got the opportunity to play some of the most exciting and challenging roles on the stage, like Louis in Tony Kushner's famous play about the AIDS epidemic, *Angels in America*.

I spent so much time in the greenroom of the theater department at the Haas Fine Arts Center that it became my second, and very possibly preferred, home. It had a kitchenette, so during lunch or dinner you could often find me making mac and cheese on the stove. Whenever the janitor would come around and empty the trash at night, she'd lock the outside door behind her and tell me to turn off the lights when I left. Some nights, when I stayed especially late to work on a paper, rather than walk to my apartment at two a.m., I'd sleep on the couch because it would make it easier to show up for my eight a.m. class the next day.

I kept a collection of cereal bars, ramen noodles, and paper for printing scripts and assignments under my preferred chair in the greenroom. My friends started calling me the greenroom "hermit," but I didn't mind. I wanted to finish college so badly. I wasn't going to graduate with honors, but I was determined to be the first in my family to graduate from college. During my last three semesters at Eau Claire, I was given permission to take on additional coursework, including classes during the summer and winter breaks. I stretched myself thin, but I did it. Having attended three different schools with three different concentrations, I finally had that cap and gown in my sights.

Looking back, I shouldn't have gone to college until I was ready financially and emotionally. I don't regret going to college at all. I only wish that it didn't cost so much and that it wasn't presented as such a necessity to teenagers who have yet to taste all the possibilities life has to offer. Why should young people plunge themselves into debt before having the chance to figure out what they're most passionate about and what they want out of life? My advice? Take a year. After high school, study abroad, work a job and save up money, or learn a trade. Do something that aligns with your passions or pushes you outside your comfort zone. Heading into college with confidence and direction will make it even more special. I wasn't ready to study in college because I wasn't in a comfortable place with myself.

Standing on the sideline of the gymnasium, Mom and

Dad posed for a picture with their arms around their young-est boy, now dressed up in a cap and gown, beaming with pride as I held a bachelor's degree in my hand. They knew this was a big deal, and I felt a sense of accomplishment and pride I had never tasted before. Mom and Dad took me out to dinner to celebrate, and we spent the evening reflecting on all the challenges the last four and a half years had thrown at me. I could see in their faces what this meant to them. "We are just so proud of you, Bubby" (I know, I know, the nickname!). I knew Mom wasn't lying. I could see the hap-piness radiating from their smiles. For as hard as it had been, and for all the bumps and hoops along the way, I had done it. Now I just had to figure out what was next.

Like the embers of fireworks falling back to Earth, the celebration soon fizzled, and it was time to say goodbye to Eau Claire. I shoved garbage bags full of clothes and books into the back seat of my car and then slowly drove down Water Street, the main street next to campus, to catch one last glimpse of the places that had shaped and tested me over the last few years. I slowly rolled past the Haas Fine Arts Center, the coffee shops, the volleyball courts I'd played on in the summer, the river I'd swum in during hot sum-mer days, and finally, the late-night burrito hangout that dreaded whenever the theater kids arrived. Eau Claire had been everything I needed it to be.

A few miles down the road, I turned the Saturn onto I-94 and headed east. Snow flurries scattered across the back windshield once more, and the hills of Chippewa County slowly disappeared on the horizon.

I turned the wipers up faster to clear the snow, turned up the volume on the speakers, and gripped the steering wheel as I drove into the unknown.

Well, I thought, *let's go see what's out there.*

10

Between the Sublime and the Ridiculous

While sitting in the back of a black SUV, headed toward our umpteenth campaign stop of the day, my assistant, Emily, looked up from her phone with panic on her face. We were both scrolling through Twitter and saw the news at the same time. There were rumblings online that a few protestors might be waiting for us when we arrived at our destination. A small group of people who supported a different presidential candidate were going to show up and let me know it. Emily and I looked at each other, worried and disappointed. "It'll be okay," I reassured her, but to be honest, I wasn't so sure that was true. It was late in the campaign, and the stakes were too high for anything embarrassing or distracting to happen, even if it came from only a few vocal critics on the sidewalk with a camera. In the political echo chamber, that's enough for a news story these days.

The car rolled to a stop just short of the entrance as we blasted "Shake It Off" by Taylor Swift for the tenth time to pump ourselves up for whatever potential unpleasantness awaited us outside. I was hosting events by myself at this point in the campaign—Peter was usually somewhere on the other side of the country holding an event too. I wished that he could've been there, but I knew I was ready to face this head-on. Emily squeezed my hand. We knew who we were, what we believed in, and why we were out on the trail doing what we were doing—nobody was going to take that away from us.

"All right, let's do this," I said as I knocked on the window twice, letting the staff outside know that I was ready. The door opened. "Hey, there he is!" one person shouted as the group of protestors quickly approached us. "Hey! Buttigieg! F*&% you!" one man yelled, lunging uncomfortably close to my face. I looked over my shoulder for Emily—it was our routine for me to wait while she maneuvered her wheelchair around the vehicle and up over the curb before we entered a building together. Emily waved me off: "Go! Just go! Get inside!" I was burning red.

And then I heard it. The sound of someone hocking a big mouthful of spit. Just as I registered what was happening, the wad of saliva hit me square in the face, then dripped from my forehead, down over my glasses, and onto my cheek. Once our staff guided me inside, I stopped to wipe off my glasses on the only thing I had to use that wouldn't draw too much attention to what had just happened: the inside of my blazer. There was already a line of people waiting to greet me the moment I walked inside. Their smiles indicated they had heard everything but were ready, like I was, to pretend it had never happened. I chuckled through a forced smile as I wiped a stranger's spit from my glasses and face, and greeted the anxious room. "Well, hello there, everyone! How're we all doing tonight?" The mood in the room immediately lightened.

The show must go on, right? So I moved on.

I'd grown up with bullies my entire life. I knew how it felt when someone knocked me down a peg and how their meanness and name-calling could bring a cloudy end to an otherwise sunny day. The thing was, I wasn't that scared little kid on the back of the bus anymore. I didn't worry about what other people thought about me the way I had in seventh-grade geography class. I'd collected enough bumps and bruises on the road to acceptance, especially the ones I'd inflicted upon myself, to know that I didn't need to allow anything to hurt me unless I chose to let it. Obviously, what they did wasn't right, and that behavior shouldn't be tolerated, but sometimes you need to let go in order to fight another day. I wasn't going to let a few mean people on a sidewalk affect this day, this campaign, or how I felt about myself.

Campaigning for president is about as tough as it gets in

politics, especially for an outsider campaign like ours. When I would take questions from reporters or sit down for television interviews, I'd often get asked the question: "You're *just* a teacher. What prepared you for presidential politics?" I knew people like me (young, nonpolitical, artsy, a middle school teacher) didn't typically appear in the big-time political arena, so I knew what was behind that question. What they were trying to ask was, *What makes you think someone like you belongs and can survive here?*

"Well," I'd say, "I have a degree in theater, and I taught middle school, so I can do anything!" They'd laugh, but I was serious.

Life had thrown a lot at me, that's for sure. Odd jobs, curious hobbies, book smarts, barn brains . . . and survival instincts—whether out of the back of a car or in a foreign language on the other side of the world. All those ups and downs had given me the grounding, strength, and courage I needed to survive the brutal but inspiring challenge that is national politics. My path hadn't been straight (*ba dum tss!*), and at times, I thought it was going to break me. Those experiences, though, all added up to something, even when I thought I had collected nothing along the way. Each lesson shaped me in different ways, leaving me with the patience and wisdom I needed to thrive.

When you're growing up, it often feels like everyone is pushing you toward the finish line as fast as they can, saying, "You just have to finish and then the next thing will be better!" Whether it's getting to the next level in karate or piano lessons, jumping from JV to varsity sports, competitive extracurricular activities, high school, or college, we tend to rush people, and ourselves, on to the "next big thing," without taking time to appreciate where we're at and what we've learned along the way. In college, there is this false promise of immediate success after you graduate, and the problem with hurrying toward the finish line is that, for many of us, that line is actually just a very steep and rocky cliff. After a lifetime of learning how to be a student, you're now expected to make entirely different sorts of decisions for yourself. The moment I left Wisconsin, I felt like Wile E. Coyote in a Looney Tunes cartoon, chasing the Road Runner right off the edge of that rocky cliff with an expensive degree in my hand. But then I looked down, and there was nothing below me.

Meep meep! *Whoosh.*

The truth is, there's no need to rush, and there's no specific formula for "success" in life, since that word means different things to everyone. That's why some people reacted so strongly to my story on the campaign trail. It wasn't the typical narrative for someone in the political world. Many people in Washington spend their whole lives trying to get a foot in the door, and once they do, they do everything they can to climb the ladders of power and success. Many people in politics knew they wanted to be there from a young age, so they made specific and calculated choices in order to build the "right kind" of résumé that would impress people in Washington. My story was very different. It was bumpy, heartbreaking, and difficult. But it got me to where I am today.

There's no need to decide your career—the one they tell you you're supposed to have for the rest of your life (also a myth)—when you're in middle or high school! It's so much more important to focus on being a kid, and to soak up as much of the adventure of youth as possible! I believed the myth of following a very narrow and specific path to success, and I beat myself up along the way when I thought I fell short. I took extra classes in college, including winter and summer semesters, and busted my tail to graduate as close to the four-year mark as possible, because that's what I was told measured your success. And then what? Whether it had taken me three or six years to graduate, I still had to enter the real world, just like everyone else. I realized that those made-up deadlines don't matter. You can set yourself up for success right now by focusing on the things that inspire you and keep you curious.

I'll never forget the day a teacher asked my ninth-grade class to prepare research on schools and degrees we might be interested in for college. At the time, I was curious about marine biology, and I had discovered a program in San Diego, California. After sharing my discoveries and passions with my teacher, she looked at me and said, "I don't know, Chasten. That doesn't seem like you. Maybe aim a little lower." Who extinguishes the fire of curiosity in a kid like that? Do me a favor and never listen to people like her. Spend less time worrying about other people's paths and opinions of your dreams and, instead, find the things that inspire you to be a better version of yourself. There's a popular saying out there: "If you enjoy what you do, you'll never work a day in your life." That's *sort of* true. At the very least, it makes life more meaningful. So focus on figuring out what you *enjoy* first.

For me, I found joy in theater education. I had spent a few years fumbling around in nursing school, and when I'd discovered that wasn't for me, I thought maybe social work was the right path to a gratifying and helpful career. In the end, that wasn't right either, so I jumped around to other possibilities, but none of them fit. I was ready to give up—I figured my compass was broken. But then my UWEC advisor, Dr. Chapman, taught a course that required students to adapt school curricula into theater exercises in order to teach lessons through drama. Afterward, the instructor would help participants process what they had learned through that pretend situation. I loved the class and quickly realized that the way I wanted to help people was by teaching, particularly in a creative way.

Not long after I left Eau Claire, I landed a teaching job in Milwaukee at First Stage, one of the nation's premier children's theaters. I was thrilled: I'd gotten a position doing exactly what I'd gone to school to do. I knew this was the foot in the door I needed. In order to supplement my teaching income, I applied at the Starbucks around the corner from where I was renting a small, dark, spider-infested bedroom in a friend's basement. Early mornings and long weekends at the coffee shop tested my patience, and the students at the theater academy pushed me to be creative and adaptable. I learned everything I could at First Stage, and then it was time to move on.

Ready for the next adventure, I packed up and moved south to Chicago in search of something bigger. I swapped spiders for roaches in a one-bedroom apartment so close to the elevated train line that the lights of the subway cars would fill my bedroom and shake my bed anytime a train went by (which I quickly learned was about every two minutes). I spent two years in Chicago Public Schools substitute teaching until I knew for a fact that the spitballs, taunts, and teenagers laughing at my shoes were no match for the sense of accomplishment I felt when I helped a student find that "aha" moment in the classroom. So I enrolled in graduate school at DePaul University and got a master's degree in education.

Right around this time, I fell in love with a brilliant and handsome mayor who was regularly traveling through Chicago on his way to drill for the Navy Reserves: Pete. He is a polyglot (he speaks many languages), and he impressed me on those first dates in coffee shops and Thai restaurants by easily switching between French and Arabic as he dazzled me with stories about his world travels or public service. German was one language he hadn't studied, and I could tell he was just as fascinated by my adventures out in the world as I was by his. It was refreshing to meet someone who asked a lot a questions, and I could tell he was genuinely curious about my passions and career—teaching middle school, it turned out, was very different from his long days in the mayor's office. We hit it off fast.

Our childhoods and educational paths were very different, but we were both in jobs that were rooted in service to others. We had both, in our own ways, explored the world enough to make decisions about how we wanted to help and who we wanted to be. My early years of struggling to fit in and belong in school ultimately brought me back there as a teacher, in hopes that I could make the next generation's experience a better one. And, of course, I had found the strength to come out and be myself.

I believe that some of the ways Peter sees the world, and approaches service, come from a different early experience, especially the horrible years of repression he encountered when he was younger. I couldn't have stayed in the closet as a teenager any longer than I did, and after I busted down the closet door, I spent years battling depression suicidal thoughts, and coming to terms with the internalized homophobia that made me feel worthless. Peter, on the other hand, felt many of those same feelings but knew he had to stay in the closet if he wanted to succeed (members of the military weren't allowed to be out until 2011).

It wasn't until Peter was seeking reelection as mayor of his hometown that he decided to share his story in an essay published in the local newspaper titled "Why Coming Out Matters." At the time, the then governor of Indiana, Mike Pence, passed a bill making it legal for individuals and businesses to discriminate against LBGTQ+ people so long as they cited their religion as justification. I can only imagine how dark and isolating it must have felt for Peter, having to hide his truest self for so many years, and how freeing it must have been to no longer care what those people thought about who he was or whom he loved.

Peter and I took very different paths to coming out, but there's no right or wrong choice here, because there is no right or wrong way to come out. When you're ready, you're ready. I think Peter knew he was destined for great things, but he also knew that his potential wasn't set in stone: he felt like the secret he was keeping could set him back or stall him forever, just like I had felt growing up only a few hours north of him in Northern Michigan. I felt like being gay was eating me alive from the inside, and if I didn't let it out, it would destroy me. For many, it's not as simple as saying, *Let's see what happens!* Even though I endured a lot of pain after I came out, I was able to be fully myself while living through it. Not everyone gets even that.

Although Peter didn't come out until he was in his

thirties, he was able to do so on his terms and in a way that made him feel better about sharing his story, especially for the people who looked to him for reassurance that South Bend was a welcoming city. Most of the country knows how impressive his résumé is. He'd become an expert on national security when I still probably couldn't have used the phrase in a sentence (now I can, and on live TV!). I don't feel jealous of what Peter has—the only thing I find myself envying, in tougher moments, is his certainty that things will always work out. He's an insufferable optimist.

If figuring out when and how to come out hadn't been as mentally taxing as it was on me for so many years, then perhaps figuring out the other parts of my life would have been easier for me as well. Things might have been a bit steadier. Just by living in one place and studying at one university for four years, Peter had developed stronger connections to his studies, his friendships, and his community than I had. I was always moving around, which made it harder to develop strong ties and concentrate on learning. Peter had remained focused on the possible, not the personal, while I'd mostly been running from myself. Thank goodness our two paths eventually crossed.

Navigating the hard parts of life was easier with Peter by my side. I had found someone who was willing to have tough conversations and happy to let me cry on his shoulder when I needed to. I don't think I truly began to believe in myself until Peter came along, looked me in the eye, and said, "You know *I* believe in you, right?" I was so wrapped up in the ways I felt broken and unaccomplished, but he was so wrapped up in the ways I made him feel loved and complete. Peter had always been driven by success, and from a young age, he believed that success and service to country was incompatible with being out or finding love. When the opportunity for advancement appeared, he took it. But when the opportunity for love appeared, he often ran the other way. By the time we met, he, too, was ready to ask for help.

One of the things I love most about Peter is his constant daydreaming—how he's always thinking about other people, or ways to be helpful, or a random line of poetry that our walk through the woods just inspired. (He quotes books; I quote movies.) I love having an up-close seat to the way he sees the world. Sometimes I'll poke him when it seems he's gone off somewhere else in his head. "Hey," I'll ask, "where'd you go?" Very early on in our relationship, he'd just say sorry and come right back to me with a smile. But with encouragement ("Hey, what's going on in that head of yours?"), his "sorry" slowly evolved into, "I don't know how to put it into words," which, with more time and love and trust, became, "Chasten, can I tell you something?" I believe it's those honest exchanges that prepared us for what came next in our lives, even if we had no idea that our lives were going to change so significantly or so fast. Though we're very different people in some ways, we both have the same approach to the other's problems: "I love you. How can I help?"

On the day of our wedding, our pastor described how our lives would take us on journeys both awe-inspiring and downright laughable. He said, "Love lives in that space between the sublime and the ridiculous. Love lives in that space between poetry and prose; between art and science; between the divine and the mundane. Love lives in that space between claiming our high calling and doing the dishes." He was so right. There would be highs and lows of varying difficulty and silliness ahead. We'd dine in the White House and then come home to a family of squirrels that had somehow taken shelter in the laundry baskets in our twins' nursery. We'd travel overseas representing the United States on an official presidential delegation and spend our Sundays buying paper towels and dish soap at Target. We'd wipe away tears of unbridled love as we held our precious newborn children in our arms and still disagree over whose turn it was to change the diaper at four in the morning. There would be nastiness in politics but inspiration in service, and profound love in our growing family. Life really is a mixture of the sublime and the ridiculous.

And, it turns out, love—whether it comes from someone else or from inside yourself—can make all the difference.

A Scoop of Advice

I am often asked the question: "If you could go back and tell your younger self one thing, what would it be?" I think people ask this question a lot because it's a tricky one. What would my younger self be able to change if I could jump back in time and bring with me one little nugget of wisdom? Am I allowed to say only one sentence, or is this more of a "sitting on a park bench with my arm around Young Me's shoulder as we stare off into the sunset" sort of situation? Will I appear like a ghost in *A Christmas Carol,* or am I just . . . an older me (but still, like, fun and cool)? As a theater nerd heavily invested in the development and execution of a story, I have a lot of questions!

Knowing younger Chasten, he's probably not going to take to the ghost thing very well. The park bench, however, could be a great setting for a helpful talk, but I should probably bring some ice cream.

Assuming Young Me doesn't run screaming as I approach and tell him that I am from the future, I'd first say: "Hey, guess what? You make it."

"I *what*?" Younger Me most certainly asks in a sassy tone.

"I know you're questioning whether it's going to be okay to be who you are. And whether you're going to be able to hush those voices in your head that tell you you're unworthy of love or happiness or friendship. I know how loud those voices can be. I know how painful this world can feel when it seems you have to hide yourself from it. I know how much you're hurting, and I promise you that you will make it. And you will be happy."

"Hmm. If you're going to keep talking, can I have that ice cream?" Younger Me demands (because of course he does). So, we both dig into our ice cream. (Younger Me prefers cotton candy, while Older Me settles for Cherry Garcia.)

"It might seem impossible right now, but there will come a day when you will stop caring about what all these kids think about you. And that secret you're doing your very best to hide will one day be the thing that helps you make a tremendous impact in this world. In fact, once you embrace that secret, you're going to fall in love, both with yourself and with someone else."

"Oh, gross!" Younger Me says.

"I know!" I laugh. "A few times, actually. And you're going to get your heart broken into a million little pieces, and that's just fine, because you'll pick yourself up, glue your heart back together, and be better for it. And then you'll go do impressive things that mean so much to so many people. And you really do meet a prince."

"Okay, now I know you're not real."

"Well, he's technically a mayor, but stick with me. You'll see the world together, and just when you feel like adventure has lost its excitement, you'll get a phone call from an adoption agency, and—"

"Whoa, whoa, whoa," Younger Me exclaims. "I think I've heard enough today, thank you." With his ice cream eaten, he'll look disappointedly at the bottom of the dish before getting up from the bench. "Well, thanks for that. I don't know if I believe in time travel, but I appreciate your time." And off he'll walk.

I think about conversations with my younger self often. What I would give to be able to go back and whisper in my ear, *These people aren't worth your time, just get through this!* or *Trust your gut, you know who you are!* Nowadays, these hypothetical conversations I play out in my head morph into what I want my kids, Penelope and Gus, to hear. I guess the most important thing I want them to know is that they are loved, and that they are and will be loved for exactly who they are.

I hope you feel that way too. I hope you know that you

belong, even if your immediate surroundings are telling you otherwise, or even if you're doubting yourself. There are a lot of people out here rooting for you, I promise.

If you're struggling with feelings of exclusion, you are not alone. *You are never alone.* School can be a tough place for everyone, regardless of your gender or identity, but it's important to know that there are always people ready to listen and talk with you. I know that it can feel overwhelming to keep moving forward when your peers or community make you feel invisible or unwanted. You are not defined by your surroundings. You are not defined by those people. Even when you feel unempowered, believe me, you get to decide what matters. You get to write your story, not them.

If you're not a member of the LGBTQ+ community but consider yourself an ally, I hope you'll reflect on how you can contribute to a world in which your peers never have to feel like there isn't space for them.. You have so much power with your words and actions—please use them well!

I know you are capable of wonderful things. I can't wait to see the world we build together.

Acknowledgments

To say this book has been an odyssey would be an understatement. Just as the creative wheels were starting to turn on the writing process, our precious twins, Penelope and Gus, came barreling into our lives and changed it all for the better. Of course, newborn twins meant a few delays in the writing process. My gratitude is boundless for the stellar teams at Atheneum and Simon & Schuster who continued to believe that this story was valuable and worthy of telling, even if it meant waiting. It really does take a village, and I am so happy to have been in this one over the last two years.

Thank you to publisher Justin Chanda for seeing the importance of this type of YA book from the very beginning. I am grateful for Atheneum publicist Alex Kelleher, who championed the vision that this book should inspire conversations far and wide as we seek to build empathy and tolerance from coast to coast. Thank you to Greg Stadnyk for the beautiful and inviting cover, and to Irene Metaxatos for the equally charming interior design. I am so grateful for the careful copyediting eye of managing editor Jeanine Ng and Cindy B. Nixon, as well as the detailed proofreading of

Bara MacNeill, and paralegal Vicky Wong. Many thanks to writer Sarah Durand for her guidance and consultation on adapting my previous written work for a younger audience. Thanks also to Anum Shafqat for her assistance to editor Julia McCarthy.

I am eternally grateful for my editor Julia McCarthy. I never doubted for a second that Julia valued my opinion or vision for this book. Working alongside someone as funny and talented as Julia made surmounting the peaks of this writing journey a breeze. There is a constant fear of mine in public life that people will stop telling you what they think or challenging you to grow. I didn't have to worry about that with Julia. She made me a better and more honest writer in the process by pushing me to take time and reflect meaningfully on my youth, to think deeper about what those experiences meant for me, and to work harder, draft after draft, because she shares a similar passion for stories with purpose. I am as thankful for her professionalism and talent as I am for her friendship.

Thank you to my management team—Eliza DeVone, Sejin Park, and Jon Liebman at Brillstein Entertainment Partners—and my literary agent, Cait Hoyt, at CAA for encouragement and patience while I figured our author-dad life!

Many thanks to the friends and allies who read through early drafts and provided helpful guidance and perspective. I am so grateful that you took the time to help shape this story. Thank you to Kristie Bach, Jennifer Chapman, Michael Halle, Anthea Hartig, Mary Heim, Danielle Hirshberg, Betsy Hodges, Swati Mylavarapu, Kal Penn, Courtenay Raymond, Sonal Shah, Emily Voorde, and Garret Wood-Sternburgh.

I am fortunate to have such a loving and supportive group of friends who helped me sift through decades of stories and memories from our younger years. I'm so grateful for those long chats around the campfire or hikes through the woods where we discussed details of our childhoods that were sharper and more difficult than they needed to be. We didn't know how crucial those relationships were when we were younger but thank goodness our kids will now know when to speak up and what to say. Hannah Bach, Erin Bernhard, Caroline Gillard, Aubrey Jabour, Eddie Neve, Trevor Pelon, Aven Purcell, Kathy Staats, Connor Sweeney, and Hannah B. Sweeney—I am so grateful for your friendships.

To my parents for telling their stories and fact-checking mine. I couldn't do any of this without your love, inspiration, and cheerleading. I am so lucky to be your son.

And to Peter and the twins. Thank you for your patience while I stepped away from the very precious time we have together as a family to write this book. My world is made more colorful and meaningful because I am loved by you. Penelope, Gus—I hope that one day these words will still mean something, and that I will have made you proud because I wrote them. I am so happy I get to be your dad.

Photos Through the Years

Top left: Me and Mom

Above: Uncle Gene's cabin outside Baraga, Michigan

Left: Five-year-old me, rocking the denim-on-denim fashion of the 1990s

Left: Lucky the Goat. That was his name, but at the time, he was also the GOAT.

Right: Six-year-old me serving early '90s Northern Michigan woodland realness

Left: A young angler and, dare I say, fashion icon

Below: At the Northwestern Michigan Fair during my freshman year. Yes, those are cowboys on my shirt.

Right: The infamous Mitsushitzu

Below: The exchange student in Berlin, Germany

Right: My high school graduation. Yes, those are bowling medals.

Left: My grandmother Wanda and me at my high school graduation

Facing page: My first time in Washington, D.C., just before leaving for Germany

Below: Dad and me fishing in the Upper Peninsula of Michigan

IN THIS TEMPLE
AS IN THE HEARTS OF THE PEOPLE
FOR WHOM HE SAVED THE UNION
THE MEMORY OF ABRAHAM LINCOLN
IS ENSHRINED FOREVER

Above: On the campaign trail

Right: The night Pete won the Iowa Caucus

Reflection Questions

Dear reader, teacher, or parent,

   As a former teacher, one of my favorite aspects of a book study was the thought-provoking discussion a text inspired. I loved watching those aha moments happen as students spoke in class or around the lunchroom table. It is my hope that the following questions will provide you an opportunity for further conversation about the text, as well as a chance to reflect within yourself   and as a community or family.

   Not all these questions are for everyone, and that's okay. Similarly, not all the answers to these questions should be shared with others unless you are ready to do so. We are each on our own journey. I hope that with compassion and patience, we can provide one another the respectful space necessary for a conversation rooted in the belief that everyone deserves to feel celebrated and loved for who they are. Equally, it is my hope we can all think about what more we can do as allies to make sure that equality and acceptance reaches everyone.

   Yours in allyship,
   Chasten

Before having tough conversations, it is always important to think of safety. In order to discuss potentially difficult topics, all parties have to be willing to engage respectfully.

1. Authenticity requires vulnerability, and sometimes people feel they must choose between being authentically themselves and being accepted. Chasten describes how his younger self feared being honest about his identity might be perceived by others as being weak. In your opinion, is vulnerability a sign of weakness? In what ways might it be a strength?

2. Chasten explains how it wasn't always easy to feel different from his peers, even when they shared similar interests and identities. Have you ever struggled with being your truest self around others? If yes, what does it feel like to not be seen as a whole person with unique differences or abilities? If no, what gives you the confidence to be uniquely *you*?

3. Chasten describes a battle that played out in his head as he debated whether he should be his true self around his peers or focused on blending in. Why might we put pressure on ourselves to fit in rather be our authentic self? What are some ways in which you can be kinder to yourself about being unique or about not being the same as everyone else?

4. Is fitting in a myth? Chasten talks about how he wishes his younger self would have known it was okay to be different. If you could go back in time, what would you tell your younger self about the idea of "fitting in?" Who do you think we are "fitting in" for? What do you think matters more: authenticity or popularity?

5. Think about how Chasten's opinion of himself changed once he leaned into his differences. What ultimately helped him believe in himself?

6. What makes it easier to be vulnerable around your friends and family than it is to be vulnerable around strangers or acquaintances? How does it feel when you're able to be your truest self?

7. How has your sense of identity changed over time? Are you more confident now than when you were younger? If yes, what inspired that confidence? If no, what might be getting in your way?

8. Have certain beliefs about yourself or your community changed over time? What prompted those changes?

9. How can you make sure that you're being the best ally to yourself each and every day?

10. What do you think about the term "coming out"? Should LGBTQ+ people have to "come out" to their peers and community?

11. Talking about our fears or feelings with friends can sometimes be awkward. Chasten was lucky to have some very good friends who showed up for him and made space to talk about those feelings of isolation and fear, even when it was difficult. How might you let your friend know you're there for them should they every need to talk about something difficult or worrisome?

12. How can you show up for someone who is struggling to build their confidence? What specific things might you say to put their worries at ease?

13. What might be a helpful thing to say when someone shares something vulnerable with you?

14. Take a moment to think about the term "intersectionality": the complex, cumulative way in which the effects of multiple forms of discrimination (such as racism, sexism, and classism) combine, overlap, or intersect, especially in the experiences of marginalized individuals or groups. How does intersectionality relate to marginalization within the LGBTQ+ community?

15. How might our awareness of intersectionality change our perspective of the experiences of people in any marginalized group?

16. What does the word "ally" mean to you? Who were some of Chasten's allies?

17. Allyship requires action. We might think of ourselves as friendly and accepting of others, but allyship can't just take place in our thoughts. Whether it's at school, on a sports team, or in any other group you belong to, think about some ways in which you can contribute to a more inclusive environment. What might be missing in those spaces? How can you be an ally and a leader?

18. Chasten grew up around some people who held very different beliefs about his identity and humanity. How did Chasten help change their minds? Are there people in your life who share opposing beliefs as you? How might you be able to change hearts and minds regarding people in marginalized communities?

19. It's more constructive to disagree with opinions, not people, and approaching a conflict from a place of good intentions and empathy is a great way to start a conversation about opposing views. How might you share your differing opinion with someone in a way that preserves empathy?

20. How should you respond to rumors that someone is part of the LGBTQ+ community but hasn't come out?

21. Is it problematic for potential allies to expect LGBTQ+ peers to ask them nicely for their allyship?

22. How can you respond when you hear someone make a harmful or bigoted comment? What if the comment came from someone you consider a friend? Would you speak up? How can we hold one another accountable without damaging our friendships?

23. How do you think you should respond when seeing harmful comments online? Think back to questions about allyship. How can you support someone without escalating an interaction or furthering an argument?

If you have any more
questions about things like allyship,
bullying, and coming out, organizations such
as the Trevor Project can provide additional
resources. You can visit thetrevorproject.org for
more information or to connect to a crisis
counselor at any day or time, from
anywhere in the US.